The Financial Planner's
Guide to
Client Consideration

Hal Rogers

outskirtspress
DENVER, COLORADO

Outskirts Press, Inc.
http://www.outskirtspress.com

ISBN: 978-1-4787-3814-5

Outskirts Press and the "OP" logo are trademarks belonging to Outskirts Press, Inc.

PRINTED IN THE UNITED STATES OF AMERICA

The Financial Advisor's Guide to Client Consideration

By

Harold J. "Hal" Rogers, CFP
Senior Advisor
Gold Tree Financial, Inc.
President
Adroit Advisors, Inc.

Harold J. Rogers, CFP®, Senior Advisor, Gold Tree Financial, Inc., and President, Adroit Advisors. Advisory services offered through Investment Advisors, a division of ProEquities, Inc., a Registered Investment Advisor. Securities offered through ProEquities, Inc., a Registered Broker-Dealer, Member, FINRA & SIPC. Gold Tree Financial, Inc. is independent of ProEquities, Inc. hal@gtfjax.com

Dedication

To Nana, who cared more about my success than anyone else who wouldn't profit from it.

"Beth Ann is a sweet girl and she loves Pop Pop!"

(My five year old granddaughter asked me to put that in my book…
All grandfathers in the world will understand!)

TABLE OF CONTENTS

INTRODUCTION

"Client Consideration" is not found painted on a financial advisor's office marquee. If it were, I might question its validity. Client consideration is like real religion – it isn't a thing you do; it is how you do everything else. Yet, we can't depend on good intentions and expect it to just fall into place. Client consideration is a culture in which a financial planner functions while intentionally doing specific things for the benefit of his or her clients. My experience is that an examination of this culture will reveal opportunities for valuable results obtainable for clients and for advisors.

I am convinced that client consideration that is limited to offering beverages and striving for that nebulous objective of "putting their interest ahead of our own" (more to follow on this) will likely fall short. These efforts fail to transfer well-meaning sentiments into meaningful efficacious client experience. As we progress I think you will see that the most relevant yardstick by which we can actually measure results, is the extent to which our efforts translate into client benefits; the measurement of those benefits is the measurement for practice success.

"The Financial Advisor's Guide to Client Consideration" will address those things which make us more successful, but we will define our success both in terms of benefits to our clients first, and then in terms of our personal earnings. I am going to encourage you to look for methods that will see that these two results are generated simultaneously. We will isolate specific concepts we can embrace and practical steps we can take that manifest a culture in our offices for ourselves and our staff that provides real value to clients. That value can then be measured by the extent to which these things become real solutions and...

1) Work better for our clients than what they were already doing

2) Register valid internally for us, thereby increasing our self-confidence, and...

3) Collaboratively make us more successful financially.

The standards, systems, and procedures i.e. the practices utilized in any business are the product of the mindset of the owners, managers, and employees of that business. Therefore, we are going to delve into the underlying mindset that translates into client consideration, and thereby makes for a more successful financial advisory practice. Then we will look at specific practices, that can make any financial advisor more valuable, or better yet, indispensable to their clients.

Before you read further, however, it is imperative to understand one thing clearly. Client consideration is not a gimmick; it isn't something you do to try to convince people to buy from you. *Client consideration has to be legitimate or it isn't considerate!* Simon Sinek illustrates this point clearly with his quote from "Start With Why"[1], "Authenticity means that everything you say and everything you do, you actually believe!"

---

1   "Start With Why": by Simon Sinek. Penguin Books Ltd. 2009

Additionally, for the purposes of this book, I am going to distinguish between a financial advisor and a financial planner. A financial advisor provides input in a limited section of a client's financial arena. A financial advisor may provide tax return preparation services; sell investments or insurance, or offer advice or consultation in any other limited portion of a client's overall financial dealings.

In addition to the above, a financial planner may provide comprehensive services generally related to financial, tax, and/or estate planning, incorporating a significantly broader spectrum of a client's financial world. These services could include, but would not be limited to:

1) Integrating financial, tax, and estate planning concepts into the design and implementation of an overall financial plan.

2) Incorporating specific distribution strategies into the design of an asset allocation model (This would be done before any funds are deposited into an investment account.)

3) Securing and utilizing information from the Tax Code and taking advantage of specific strategies for eliminating unnecessary taxes for clients

4) Integrating financial and tax planning with the client's estate plan to avoid probate, minimize income taxes, eliminate or minimize estate taxes, and prevent unintended heirs.

5) Reviewing and offering specific strategies for maximizing value in a client's liability insurance portfolio

6) Considering proper application for the use of a reverse mortgage where appropriate

7) Providing Health Care Asset Protection strategies designed to protect against lost inheritances (may or may not require the purchase of Long Term Care Insurance)

8) Incorporating plan design components that protect the client's assets from legal liability claims

9) Providing any other input that potentially improves the client's financial situation

Client Consideration includes the above concepts, ideas, and strategies, and, in doing so, can shape the culture prevalent in a financial planning practice. Therefore, a mindset geared toward comprehensive financial, tax, and estate planning, vs. selling financial products is the objective. I acknowledge that providing financial advice and selling financial products are honorable professions. In the larger picture they just aren't as valuable to clients as is more comprehensive planning, and my experience is that that isn't what clients are seeking when they visit a financial advisor's office. None-the-less, most of what is covered in this book will be valuable and relevant to financial advisors and financial planners alike.

Two final comments regarding the differentiation between financial advisory services and financial planning: First, while providing limited financial advice in the sale of financial products is valuable to clients, if it is done under the banner of "financial planning", in addition to the benefits it provides, it might actually harm clients. Clients who don't know the difference… don't know the difference. They may believe everything is just fine, while, actually, available opportunities could be overlooked, and they and their families might be exposed to substantial problems and downside ramifications that simply haven't been addressed. This is particularly egregious when the client goes home thinking, "My financial advisor has everything under control" but, in reality, there may still be much that hasn't even been addressed.

Secondly, financial advisors routinely shoot themselves in the foot financially. They have a relationship and an audience with their clients;

their clients are listening to them; and their clients have a positive mindset about them and their input. (If they didn't, they wouldn't be doing business with them.) Yet, they "make a sale" and walk away leaving tens of thousands, hundreds of thousands, even millions of dollars on the table. If a client doesn't have enough confidence in an advisor to accept input regarding all his accounts, does it really make sense to trust him with three hundred thousand dollars or a hundred thousand dollars, or even forty thousand dollars for that matter?

While some high net worth clients make it a point to spread their money over several firms with several advisors, this is more likely to be the case when each of these advisors is providing only investment management services. My encouragement to all financial advisors as to client consideration is to incorporate financial strategies into the work they do, and to expand their offering to include everything they can that relates to their clients' finances. A valuable peripheral benefit is that the more they do for their clients, the more likely it is that their clients will not have other financial advisors. This will be beneficial for their clients, and, together, clients and advisors will be more financially successful.

With those ideas as a foundation, I want to share a few basic beliefs that shape my approach to the subject of client consideration. I am not proselytizing, here. I have no investment in whether or not you, the reader, accept any of my personal beliefs. In fact, I don't suggest you accept any of them. Instead, I suggest that if I offer a concept that you think might possibly alter your thinking in a productive way, then apply it as a test. If it does anything you don't like, never use it again. If, on the other hand, it does something you like, try it again. Try it, use it until you don't like a result, and then discard it.

If you get results you like, you won't subsequently have a new "belief". You will have, instead, knowledge, because of your empirical experience. We oftentimes "believe" because someone else believed or because someone else suggested it. This often is nothing more than a succession of people who believed because someone else did. Once you have knowledge, the fact that someone else's input resulted in you testing something new will be of no relevance. Attempting something new because someone else suggested it, and gaining new knowledge will over the long term prove far more valuable than a new set of beliefs.

One last thing before we start. If you are a seasoned financial planner, most of what is in this book you already know. If you finish reading this and realize you have wasted your money, please do one of the following two things. Either give this book to a young advisor who needs it and might benefit from it, or send it back to me with your receipt, and I will give you your money back.

<u>Just mail it to:</u>   Hal Rogers
Adroit Advisors, Inc.
8596 Arlington Expressway
Jacksonville, FL 32211

Just for clarification, Gold Tree Financial, Inc. is where I do financial planning. I sold my practice in January to an up and coming star in our business, Scott Showers, but I still work with a very limited number of personal clients. Adroit Advisors is my financial advisory consulting company through which I help people in our industry.

CHAPTER ONE

The "Bubble Gum God"

Before we begin this chapter, let me lay a proper foundation. This book isn't for crooks or hucksters. Everything I say in this book is relevant to people with integrity. There may be some aspects of the business that you haven't figured out yet, but if your basic position is one of genuine honesty and integrity, and if you present yourself with honorable intent in your profession, the ideas and concepts herein should be beneficial.

All of my internal esoteric perspective can be summarized into a singular concept that I call the "Bubble Gum God" concept. Imagine a huge wad of chewed bubble gum as large as a million galaxies, stretched across the depths of space. Now imagine that someone reached out; pinched a portion of that bubble gum, pulled it down to earth and stuck it in my chair. That piece of bubble gum would mark my placement in the Universe.

Now, imagine that the process was repeated, yet from the opposite end of the bubble gum wad, and the little piece strung out from that end was stuck in your chair, marking your placement in the Universe. What is important here; is that when those pinches were pulled from that wad of bubble gum, they didn't separate from it. In each case; they left a string of bubble gum stretching out between the main piece, and the piece at the end.

In this example, there aren't two pinches, two strings, and the main wad; it is all the same piece of bubble gum, a unified entity. I believe that everything in this Universe is like that piece of bubble gum; except in my model, the chewing gum encompasses everything. *There is only one anything, and it is everything.* In my esoteric studies, I have found a foundation for this concept in several of the world's religions.

Okay, I'll agree that the example used here may appear silly; but the analogy helps to illustrate a point which might be valid, that we are not separate from each other in this world...we are unified. The validity of my previous statement and concept here is this: "If, from the beginning, my understanding was that you and I were part of the same whole, then as our paths intersected maybe I would treat you better". My sense is that there is no "them", there are no "others", there is only "Us". The vast majority of the world's problems stem from a belief in the concept of "others" i.e. duality. This basic stance allows us to function as though we are separate and unicellular from the whole. From this stems the misguided belief that my interest and your interest are unrelated, or as in "Zero Sum Game Theory"[2], that your loses are my gains.

The "Bubble Gum God" concept is relevant when working with our individual clients – it is also relevant as to the collective financial

---

2   Zero Sum Game: A game in which one participant's gains equal the other participant's losses. Example – Two people playing poker.

industry. I spent years thinking of all the other financial advisors in the world as my enemies. I feared that they were getting clients that could have been mine. Living in that belief system not only distracted my focus, but restrained my ability to offer my best services to both existing and potential clients. Today, as I have shifted my paradigm, the financial planner study groups in which I have participated have provided significant value and feedback for both me and the other members of the groups. Numerous times since coming to this realization I have flown to another financial advisor's office, or had another financial advisor visit me just to exchange ideas. In each case we spent an invaluable day sharing and learning from each other, and we both came away the better for it.

The bottom line - if I can embrace the concept that we are all on the same team i.e. that we are really all One, vs operating from an "others" or me vs. them mentality... it might have beneficial effects on my financial advisory practice. Anything that benefits another human being benefits me, and anything that makes the financial planning industry better, also benefits me!

The best scenario is one in which two people are playing golf and one asks the other, "So, who is your financial advisor?" When the second person says, "Oh, I don't have one", the first is aghast. "What? You don't have a financial advisor? What is the matter with you? Do you live in a cave? Are you brain dead? Put your clubs back in the bag. We are leaving right now. I am taking you to see my advisor this minute!" When this is the environment in your city, you will know that our industry is doing the right things and you won't have to worry about your competition!

CHAPTER TWO

Who's Interest Do I Put First?

How do we relate the Bubble Gum God concept to financial planning? This is revealed in that most important question every financial advisor must address... *"Who's interest do I put first, mine or my clients?"* Before you even address this question, let me share that I have asked this question of many advisors in a serious, "we're being honest here" conversation, and with one exception, they shared with me that this was something they struggled with in their career. You will see why as you read further. If you answer this question "your client's" or if you say, even to yourself, "sometimes I'm afraid I may let my own interest get in the way" ... while these answers are typical, both of them have to be wrong!

The flaw lies within the question itself. First, whichever way it is answered, there is something about the other answer that has attraction to it. Secondly, in certain instances, a case made for value seems to be valid from either answer chosen. In reality, the question can't be answered at all, because the question itself is ludicrous!

Consider this; if I noticed that you had a calculator on your desk, and I asked you which calculator on the desk was better at doing time value calculations, you would think my mind had slipped. If there is only one calculator, you couldn't say one was better or one was worse. With only one calculator on the desk, the question wouldn't make any sense.

If someone looked in the driveway and saw only one car, and is then asked which car in the driveway was the fastest, the question would be immediately seen as ridiculous and unanswerable. Any answer would be irrelevant because there was only one car in the driveway! The question itself is an inane question.

The question "Who's best interest do I put first, mine or my clients?" is exactly the same kind of question, because it isn't possible for an advisor to put his interest ahead of his client's, or his client's interest ahead of his own. It isn't possible because the advisor / client relationship is a relationship of perfect reciprocity. <u>Our best interest and our clients' best interest aren't alike; they aren't similar</u>...*the interest of the advisor and the client are one and the same; there is only one interest.* **<u>My clients' best interest is my best interest. Your client's best interest is your best interest. There is only one interest on the table!</u>**

> **An advisor who believes he puts his clients' best interest ahead of his own has integrity. An advisor who understands that his clients' interest and his own interest are one and the same has wisdom.**

Any action on the part on an advisor which isn't in his or her client's best interest will hurt that advisor. Either short term (psychologically), or long term (financially), or both, ultimately it will cost that advisor. Any temporary financial advantage will pale in comparison to the long-term cost. Additionally, it isn't true that it may be temporarily beneficial to the advisor. The internal damage to the advisor, that advisor's own sense of self, is brutally damaged when they knowingly do anything they sense may be contrary to their client's best interest, and that damage is immediate. It also leaves them less effective in their interaction with their next potential client because they know they aren't who they want this prospective client to think they are.

Look at the key components influencing your chances of being successful, when your next potential client walks into your office. They are:

1) Technical knowledge in the arena

2) Effective communication skills related to presenting advantageous ideas and concepts i.e. available strategies, to clients, and...

3) ***The ability to interact with that client with confidence***

1) **Technical knowledge** - This will come with training and experience, and it will continue to increase as long as you are in the business. If you are young, unless you are partnered with someone with some maturity in the business, you are working at a disadvantage, and clients who are seasoned know that. Either join up with a successful advisor or get a mentor. There is no other short term way to overcome this disadvantage. You may have the ability to function, to interact, to sell, but you

don't know what you don't know. Casey Kasem said: "Success doesn't happen in a vacuum. You're only as good as the people you work with, and the people you work for."[3]

Experienced advisors and planners will tell you that technical skills you need in this industry won't come from standard industry continuing education (CE) courses. I have found that you can score credit to meet industry requirements, but the technical programs that will provide the most valuable information for your clients generally don't come with CE credits. A good example is nationally recognized CPA, Ed Slott's IRA Advisor Training.[4] I had been in the business for twenty years when I met Ed, and I didn't know what I didn't know!

2) **Effective Communication Skills** - These are learned, practiced, and honed over time. Even if you are reasonably competent in this area, these skills will improve throughout your career.

3) **Self Confidence** - *The most important factor related to your ability to interact with your clients with confidence is your opinion of yourself, and nothing will improve this as much as the internal knowledge that you have the technical expertise noted above and that you take care of your clients! Period! No exceptions! End of story.* Perfecting self-confidence requires the intrinsic understanding that you are totally committed to serving your client well. There is no way around this. If anything is missing here, you have to maintain a front, a façade of good intentions. You have to hide the true you, the you that wants to sell something to someone. If you have integrity, anything short of perfection

---

3   http://www.allaccess.com/net-news/archive/story/123516/casey-kasem-longtime-american-top-40-host-voiceove
4   www.irahelp.com

in this component will leave you uncomfortable. If you are uncomfortable, you will not present yourself confidently to your existing or prospective clients, and a percentage of the people you meet will feel uncomfortable during their interactions with you.

This isn't rocket science. Even if what you really want is to sell the person in your office something that makes you a commission or a fee, that isn't what you are trying to convey to the person sitting across the desk from you. There is nothing wrong with selling quality products of any kind, and there is nothing wrong with getting paid to do so, but prospective clients aren't seeking a relationship with a product salesperson, and you don't want your client to see you as such. *Any attempt to disguise this intention will be transparent to some of the clients you want most, and always to yourself!*

It isn't true that the most effective way to keep people from seeing you that way is not to be that way…the **only** way to keep them from seeing you that way - is to not be that way! When there is nothing to hide, self-confidence soars! When you are truthful with yourself and the nature of your intentions, the nature and tone of your prospective client and client interactions experiences a fundamental shift in a way that nothing else can accomplish. This is what is known as a paradigm shift!

Since your client's best interest is your best interest, there is only one interest on the desk. It isn't possible, therefore, to put either one ahead of the other. The moment I do anything that would benefit me that I think might be disadvantageous to my client, I have just shot myself in the foot. Taking care of my clients is the best thing I can do for my wife, for my children, and for my grandchildren. Clients who are well served, valued, and appreciated, stay with their advisor.

Obviously that is financially beneficial to you when they retire, have rollover funds that need investing, and when they inherit money. Clients who are treated with genuine respect, are provided with effective planning strategies, and are delivered quality and appropriately positioned financial products, have total confidence in their advisor. Clients who both like and respect their advisor, will also bring their family and friends to that advisor. There is no limit to how beneficial this relationship can be.

This is very different from trying to convince my clients that for some noble, altruistic motivation, I, the "do good advisor with the white hat", am going to devote my life only to taking care of them. This is very different from trying to convince them that I would be willing to put them ahead of one of my grandchildren. However, it is totally reasonable and believable when they know that I know that taking care of them is what takes care of me and my family!

> **Any advisor, at any moment, can substantially raise his or her level of self-confidence, on the spot, by simply deciding that from this moment forward he or she will, with no exceptions, do everything possible, in every situation, to take the best possible care of his or her clients!**

CHAPTER THREE

Large Case Compensation

Making sound recommendations, providing competitively priced products and services, and taking care of our clients is considerate. So, what else is there to say on the subject?

For one thing, grasping the "one interest on the table" concept provides a peace of mind as it relates to compensation, including substantial compensation. I have talked to several financial advisors who have confided in me that they feel guilty when they earn more than an average amount of compensation on a case. The money itself makes them feel this way. When I hear this, I tell them the story about a client I had a number of years ago. We'll call him Bob.

Bob had consulted with two financial advisors before coming to me. They had given him sales material on a number of different financial products, but he was not satisfied with what they had told him, so, fortunately for him and for me, he decided to give me a try.

In our first meetings, I spent some time with Bob and got to know and understand him. I didn't ask him to complete a risk-tolerance assessment; we didn't discuss any financial products; and I didn't make any sales pitches. He talked; I listened. Bob told me about his deceased wife, who was Japanese and about the wonderful years they had shared before she died. I also talked to Bob about my eight children and shared some of my personal experiences with him.

As I listened to Bob talk I had an epiphany. It suddenly became very clear to me that Bob was deeply concerned about money, but his concerns were different from those of most of my clients. Bob wasn't afraid of *losing his money*; he was afraid *of his money*. Bob was a simple man, but when it came to money, the very act of dealing with it, tracking it, considering the tax implications of it, and making decisions about it, were all a heavy burden for him. It was virtually impossible for Bob to make an investment decision because he didn't understand any of it. He had no financial foundation on which to base his decision; so he had done nothing!

Once I understood Bob's problem, the solution wasn't difficult, but it meant doing something I had never considered before and couldn't have imagined that I would have suggested. But, for Bob, the plan worked out perfectly. I arranged for Bob to set aside a little money for reserves, and then purchase a gift annuity for $1.3 million. In our initial discussions, Bob had shared with me that he was a widower, didn't have any heirs and had no desire to leave money to anyone in particular. The gift annuity was the perfect vehicle for Bob.

Bob later told me that from that minute, he never worried about money again. Bob got a big tax deduction, a substantial tax-advantaged check every year for the rest of his life, and a 1099 every January… and Bob was happy. No, actually, Bob was delighted! The gift annuity eliminated Bob's burden in relation to his money. Bob said to me, "You know what I like about your plan? It is simple. I really like the way you work!"

"Simple" was what Bob needed, but I only knew that because I had spent the time necessary to ask questions outside the realm of the typical data-gathering process. I *listened* to him. As a result, I was able to provide what he needed, even though he didn't know what that was. (If Bob had known what he needed, he wouldn't have hired me!)

My compensation on the case was $139,000, at that time the largest single case compensation of my career. I did not feel guilty about my earnings. I served Bob's interests, and, oh by the way, mine were served in the process.

All the time I spent with Bob prior to implementing that simple plan, all the conversations we had — could be summed up in one statement that has profound implications: I considered Bob! I was not focused on what his money could do for me. My attention was on Bob, a man who had a problem that needed to be solved.

The secret to success in our business isn't making sure we don't cheat or take advantage of our clients. The fact that we don't sell them the wrong product for a high commission isn't the point. I would like to think that at least 98% of the people in our business already function that way; that part should be automatic. It is *considering* our clients that makes us successful.

Last year, I traveled with my wife, Sandy, who was the incoming president of our Rotary club, to a Rotary International convention in Bangkok, Thailand. While there, I took an afternoon off and went exploring and found myself at a Buddhist temple. This wasn't one of the gold and glitter tourist attractions you see in the travel posters. This was a real functioning temple with monks in residence.

After strolling through the quiet gardens where everything had a meditative feel to it, I asked one of the employees if I might speak with one of the monks who resided there. (I mentioned, by the way, that if possible, I would appreciate it if he spoke English). To my delight, they set it up for me.

When the monk sat down, his first words were, "Short conversation". Then we talked. Mostly he talked and I listened. He talked about several things, but what I remember most was what he told me about "others". He told me that most of the world's problems can be traced directly to the misconception that there are "others". He said there are no others; there is only "Us". He said "others" don't exist, and all of our beliefs that they do exist, serve "Us" very poorly.

Considering our clients is nothing more complicated than recognizing that they are "Us". "Do unto others as you would have them do unto you... because they are you!" What a concept! With that idea in the forefront, it is only natural to be patient with them when they don't understand. Implementing a gentle manner because it is appreciated is not a difficult action when you consider how you would want to be treated. In that light it becomes only natural to take the time to see whether they would prefer that we explain everything, or simply just tell them what the next step needs to be. All of these things are exactly what I would respect, and appreciate, if I were sitting on the other side of the desk.

We all have needs and they all vary in some respect, but they are identical in that we all want to be considered. If we can learn to recognize the way in which we are all the same, our differences become easier to distinguish and less important. It just takes a little time, time not spent "overcoming objectives", or with "closing" clouding our perspective. They appreciate it when we talk quietly with them on matters other than financial. They warm to us when we ask questions, listen to their responses, and retain what they say.

The irony is that they are all the same in their desire for us to recognize how they come at things from different perspectives. The good news for us is that all it takes is paying a little attention to them. Nothing more than simply being alert and aware of them is required... this is how we begin to understand them, and how we know where they are likely to be in their thought processes. That is how we know the answer before we introduce an idea we would like them to accept.

After implementation, Bob and I met regularly at my office, but we never discussed money again...there was no need. Instead, he and I talked about his work before he retired as a research scientist. He shared with me his experiences living in Japan and talked about his beloved wife, Aiko. After Bob's health failed, I went to the health care facility where he lived (and had no trouble affording) and just hung out with him, and occasionally gave him a ride to the drug store. (I still remember that Bob had never heard the term "hanging out" and thought that was pretty neat!)

I hope this somewhat lengthy but poignant introduction into the idea of client consideration will cause you not to just think outside the sales box, but to permanently move outside the sales box. I hope this moves you to forget everything you ever learned about power phrases, overcoming objections, and closing. If it does; it will prepare you for the ideas that follow, ideas you should be able to use to benefit your clients in future meetings.

CHAPTER FOUR

Where is Your Client... Emotionally?

In my thirty plus years as a financial advisor, I have identified what I believe to be the single greatest detriment to the chances of implementation during a financial recommendation for our clients. Let's see if you concur.

I often ask financial advisors, "What is the primary concern a prospective client has when they walk into your office the first time?" The standard answers are, "They are concerned with outliving their money" or "They are afraid they might lose money in investments that I recommend".

I used to think this as well... now I know better. How do I know? I asked them. The fear of outliving their money might be the primary concern of retirement age people in America, but, based on my experience, it isn't what is foremost on their mind as they're walking into my office for the first time. Secondly, they aren't afraid I will lose their money for them because at that moment, *they have no intention of doing any business with me.*

Over the last two years, during the first meeting with a prospective client, after things got settled down a little and everyone was comfortable, I have asked each of them this question. "What did you talk about in the car on the way to my office today that you wouldn't say in front of me?" The single most common answer... the wife blurts out, "He said we weren't going to buy anything!"

In the first trip to your office, your prospective clients are fearful that you are going to try to sell them something. They are anxious that they will be subjected to a sales pitch. The only way to get past this is to not give them one, and you can be confident that this approach will be 100% effective in alleviating that fear!

The feedback validating what I am saying here is fairly commonplace. We do a monthly social in my office for clients and guests. It might be a wine tasting, or an ice cream social; one time I even cooked quesadillas for everyone. At the end of one of our socials, a guest came up to me and said, "Hal, may I tell you something?" I said, "Sure, Barbara, what's up?" Kind of sheepishly she confided in me, "Do you know what Bill and I thought when we came here tonight? We thought you were going to try to sell us something!"

What Barbara didn't know was that, other than a two-minute market update and economic commentary, we never talk business at our socials. If a guest walks up to me during the evening and says, "So, Hal, exactly what do you do here?" even though he's asking, he is mentally, and more importantly, emotionally primed for a "sales pitch". His whole psyche can be poised to resist. However, my reply, is, "Jack, I am drinking wine tonight…but, if you will give me a business card, I will be happy to call you tomorrow and fill you in!" Then I ask him about himself, his job, his family, etc.

The look of surprise and relief on their faces when I respond with consideration instead of a sales pitch is always incredible. Not only that, but when I call the next day and address his question, there is absolutely no resistance. Why? Because I considered him at the social and provided him nothing to resist. There was no sales pitch!

Make certain your first time visitors know very early in that initial meeting that you are going to talk, attempt to find out what they are looking for, and give them the opportunity to know something about your processes. Also, you want to communicate to them that they need to determine if they would feel good about engaging you, and that you are going to determine if they meet the criteria necessary for you to take them on as new clients.

Your clients will feel much more considered if they understand that they met the criteria to become your clients than they will begrudgingly letting you talk them into becoming your clients. I've never found anyone who does this better than the Fross Brothers at Fross & Fross in The Villages, just south of Ocala, Florida. Their Platinum Advisors Marketing book, "Members Only"[5] does a wonderful job of showing advisors how to create, develop, and convey this concept. If you read the book, make sure you don't use the concept fraudulently – it must have integrity. In other words, your actions have to be genuine. If you never elect to not take someone as a client, don't try to create the impression that you do.

Using "Members Only" as a guide, for prospective clients, I use

---

5   "Members Only" by Robert J. Sofia, Platinum Advisor Marketing 2011 - http://www.platinumadvisormarketing.com/

four criteria to measure whether or not I am willing to accept them as new clients:

1) **Value** – First and foremost, we have to know that we can provide value with the services we provide, that their particular situation lends itself to what we do.

2) **Chemistry** – Secondly, we have to believe we would enjoy spending time with them. Given their personality and psychological makeup, we have to feel good about participating in a long term relationship with them. This will be a marriage - the chemistry has to work.

3) **Open Mindedness** – Thirdly, we have to know they are coachable, that they are open to input and want assistance. Someone who is a "know it all" doesn't qualify.

4) **Financial** – The numbers have to make sense. It has to make sense financially, for us and for them.

If clients must like and respect you to consider doing business with you, it seems only natural that you need to like and respect them before you would consider taking them on as clients. With both as prerequisites, there is a much better chance that the relationship is going to work for both of you. The considerate thing to do is to determine this right up front so you won't waste their time or yours if it isn't going to work. Then you can go about introducing them to your way of doing business and the processes you use in your practice. There are people out there that you don't want as clients. If you don't want them as clients, you don't need to waste your time or theirs on these irrelevant details.

Once that is covered, clients want to have a good feeling about what they are getting into. The easiest way to do this is to share with them the processes you utilize on behalf of your clients. If they feel comfortable with your processes they will be comfortable with you. They are comfortable because giving them a heads up on what you already know is going to happen is considerate. Accordingly, it is more effective to help them know what to expect, than it is to pat yourself on the back trying to create a positive impression. If they like the processes, everything else will come easily.

For many of my early years in this business, I consistently failed to consider the mindset of prospective clients when I met them. I was guilty of this primarily because when meeting with a prospective client, my attention was focused on my objective of selling something, on my interest in making money (personally justified, of course, because I was working to support my family). There was nothing malicious here…it was just backwards. As a result, my presentations were dysfunctional; despite the fact that I was recommending appropriate financial products. My client presentations were unproductive because I had not yet engaged them, and my recommendations were unsuccessful because I had failed to introduce those recommendations to someone *who was in the right frame of mind to receive them.*

The problem then was (and still is for the unaware) failing to grasp a prospective client's mindset during the interactive process. Understanding that what the client thinks, feels, and takes away from this process are all developmental markers for your success – this is the game changer. When we fail to understand this, we place the cart before the horse; resulting in failure to secure engagement, or worse, failure to implement a plan that would have greatly benefited the client. Even when we are successful in getting a new client; the process is much more laborious, more challenging, and much less enjoyable when we miss these fundamental indicators.

Then comes the question, "How do we determine where they are coming from?" We can know our client's mindset by doing the simplest thing in the world...we ask them. Don't do it rhetorically. Ask them the way you would want to be asked; then wait for, and listen to their answers. "Please tell me why you would be sitting at a financial advisor's desk at 10:00 on a Tuesday morning". "In considering the use of a financial planner's services, are there any concerns on your part?" "Bill, what is there that is going on in your world that would impact what we do here that I wouldn't know to ask about?" "Tom, Mary, how much are you each involved in the day to day bill paying, and how much are you involved in the bigger picture relating to investments, insurance, tax planning, asset protection, etc.?" "Yvonne, have you ever had a negative experience with someone providing financial advice that might impact my efforts to help you?" "Scott, before we address our company and how we work, do you have any specific questions you would like me to address for you?" This question particularly helps you move directly to what your prospective client has on his or her mind if they have a burning concern. If they move directly to this concern, they are probably well on the way to becoming a client. Your only job is to properly address this issue and not run them off!

This approach has *nothing* to do with the quality of the products or the recommendations themselves. All of this is relevant before you are ever asked to provide your technical expertise. This stuff is important, no critical, before you do any financial data type fact-finding or explain anything about what you do. If the client can't "hear" what is being recommended because they are on a completely different page and you don't know it, it doesn't matter how much technical expertise you have!

How about a little test to see how you are already scoring in this area? Just ask yourself three questions:

1) How many initial meetings do you conduct a week?

2) How many financial plans do you develop a week?

3) How many financial plans do you implement a week?

If you don't like your answers, take a look at your client interactions. When you meet a prospective client are you recognizing them and where they are, or are you focused on your business objectives? Are you presenting your standardized, well-worn, repetitive comments? At each subsequent meeting with a new client, do you ask any of the following questions?

1) "Has anything come up since we last met that you would like to talk about?"

2) "Is there anything in how things are progressing so far with which you aren't comfortable?"

3) "Do you have any questions or concerns so far?"

4) "How do you feel about the process so far?"

5) "As far as you can tell to this point, are we meeting your objectives; are we moving in the right direction for you?"

Have you asked yourself these questions?

1) Where are you coming from about where your clients are coming from in client interactions?

2) Are your conversations new and fresh, spontaneous, and different with each new guest in your office?

3) Are you paying attention to them and their potential benefits?

4) Are you taking the time and effort to determine for certainty their mindset before you present anything?

It is amazing how asking basic questions like those above of them and of yourself will eliminate the small concerns that were bothering them, and often does so with the simplest explanation on your part. This paves the way for the solutions you want to provide and for which you are compensated. This helps them enter into a mindset that makes them capable of hearing what you are saying when you do get to your "plan presentation".

If you aren't considering these elements of the client interaction, it's possible that you're talking to someone who potentially can't hear you. I know - I did this for years. While focused on sales opportunities, I never knew how my clients truly felt - I never asked them!

CHAPTER FIVE

The Meaning of Life

The next concept changed my world. It answered, for me, the most basic, most fundamental question. It made sense of what previously was beyond my ability to grasp. It gave me a path; a direction to follow that systematically provided much desired results. Before I considered this idea, everything I read seemed to promise the answer on the next page; but it was never there. This understanding, whether it is valid or not, helped me see, not that I was responsible for my life (which I already believed was the case), but specifically how I was responsible for my life! It answered a whole list of previously unanswerable questions, and provided functional opportunities that, previously, I had no ability to entertain.

As I share this apparently earthshattering concept, let me suggest that I am not proposing that it is the answer to everything; that it is *the answer*. I am just telling you that it works for me better than anything I had ever considered before.

Also, I am not proselytizing here; I am not suggesting that you "believe" as I do. As I already mentioned, I suggest only that you check it out; try it; and if it works for you, use it. If it doesn't, pitch it and move on.

All of my experience to this moment tells me that life is a mirror. Life isn't like a mirror; it isn't similar to a mirror. **Life is a mirror!** A mirror is an incredible systems of perfect reflection. The reflection is both unique and non-discriminatory, and life always show us the core of our true selves. Mirrors show us…"Us"! Not to wax theological here, but if you ascribe to the existence of God, this gives that concept a whole new meaning. It shows us how that God functionally delivers us exactly the input we need and want to make improvement unique to us, personally.

Mirrors only have one function…and that function is reflection. The take away here, the beautiful thing is that *all the answers we ever wanted are always right in front of us.* The only way to change a reflection in the mirror is to change what we are showing it. You can't show a mirror a banana and have it show you a Harley Davidson motorcycle. Mirrors have no ability to do that! Therefore; if there is anything in my life (my reflection) that I want changed, I know that I must change it from within myself. Bottom line is that my reflection (what's happening in my life) will not change unless and until I change me! However, when I do change, the mirror must also change what it shows me; it still has no choice. The mirror won't show me what needs to be changed, but it will show me the results of my current thoughts, feelings, and actions. It will show me what my current reflection looks like, and that's a start!

This is a whole course of study in itself, and beyond the scope of this writing. However, the basic is this. The "cause" is the tapes I play in my head; the "effect" (say reflection) is the way my practice works. I can't "hope I make a good impression" and get the results a competent and confident professional gets. In the chapters to follow we are going to address what you can absolutely deliver (controllables) that will automatically and immediately create a greatly enhanced level of competence and confidence, those you must have to attract and serve the clients you really want.

I believed for a lot of years that I was responsible for my life; I believed that to change the events and circumstances in my life I had to change me. What was missing was exactly what it was about me that had to change. I was convinced that it was internal, and that I had the ability to change it. What I didn't know was what it was. What was it that was inside me that I would have to change to get those different results I so desperately wanted? The answer, while elusive, was stunningly simple – I had to change "the tapes I play in my head", the "way I think" i.e. my subconscious!

I had internal attitudes about EVERYTHING, and they colored all my thoughts and feelings about everything that came up. What I wasn't seeing was the never-ending march of thoughts and ideas that originated with my sense of self.

I thought my sense of everything was a result of what happened outside me. What I eventually discerned was that everything that happened outside of me was the result of the sense of everything I carried internally. I first figured this out in relation to my "judgments". I began to see what they were creating, what they were manifesting in my world.

To test the theory that this was what was happening, I picked one and consciously changed my internal picture, the tape I previously subconsciously played, in relation to a specific relationship. When I did, the relationship changed, and the actions of the person involved drastically changed! I was flabbergasted. Then I tried it on something else. It worked exactly the same way again. Soon, much in my life that had been contrary to my preferences began to shift. I could see actual results of the changes I was forcing in "the tapes I played in my head". I changed me, internally, and my life changed externally. If you don't believe that, I really don't care. It doesn't affect me whether you do or not. However, if you try it for yourself, and things change in directions you like, you won't believe it; you will know it. By the way, the moment you start playing different tapes, the results are instantaneous. When you show a mirror something different there is no time delay before it shows you a different reflection!

So how then do we bring mirrors, reflections, and good intentions full circle? Your financial advisory or financial planning practice is always a perfect reflection of you…it will constantly show you the results of your mindset, your words, and your actions. *Actually, your life and what is happening in it, will perpetually show you the ramifications of the tapes you play in your head and how you feel about what you are thinking about automatically.* It will repetitively reflect at you your effectiveness, or lack of same, and who you are in relation to your clients.

The good news is that if you don't like how your financial advisory practice is working, how your career is progressing, the results you are getting, you now have the tool needed to identify and fix the areas that you feel are lacking. That tool is client consideration, and implementing this approach will stop you from accidentally, inadvertently, making mistakes. How do we prevent these mistakes as advisors? We eliminate the things that reflect things we don't like.

The worst possible example of failure to consider a client is mentioning or discussing any financial product in the first meeting. A client is either thinking, "I wonder if I could see myself working with this person", or "I'm not going to buy anything today", and we are lauding the praises of our favorite money manager or income benefit rider. The action that causes "resistance" is "selling"! *Another way of saying this is, "the reflection of selling is resistance!" If your clients are resisting, you are selling!!! For the client consideration process to be most effective, all of the financial data and client preferences must be considered. Following this, you would need to expand on the information you've gathered, and propose a **financial strategy** to your client, before any reference to or discussion of financial products is to begin. If you were allowed to read only one page of this book, I would direct you to this one!*

1) It is necessary that an advisor facilitate a connection with his or her potential client, before attempting to determine or unveil financial problems.

2) It is imperative that that advisor recognize and unveil financial problems before attempting to present any financial strategy.

3) It is crucial that the advisor present the appropriate financial strategy before suggesting any financial product, even if the client brings it up or asks!

In my financial practice; as an alternative to a discussion about any financial product, we might introduce some generic concepts that would provide value to almost anyone. Some examples of these generic concepts might include the introduction of topics such as tax advantaged distribution strategies, preventing unintended heirs, or making sure our client's attorney isn't his or her first heir, you know... $350/

hr for six to eighteen months following the death of a family member (say probate). Building the value of your practice and what you do; may seem challenging at first without offering your standard introductory comments, but this can be done with ease, all the while having nothing to do with any financial product. Instead, lead the initial discussion with consideration first, followed by a checklist, and an explanation of potential client pitfalls observed throughout your career.

A client expecting an initial sales introduction, and instead hearing that, for as long as you have been in practice, you have never had a client walk into your office whose beneficiary designation forms were correct...and that you are going to provide custom beneficiary designation documents[6] for them, might go a long way toward building the value of your practice and what you do - but it has nothing to do with any financial product. Additionally, sharing with your client the potential for devastation to an estate, simply because accounts weren't titled correctly...and how your staff will go through a checklist of every account they have anywhere, to make certain they are all titled correctly[7], in the end will prove more motivating than making an early case for long term care insurance. This doesn't mean you won't get to financial product recommendations; it just means not bringing them into the conversation where they don't belong.

This approach conveys a message other than how much money you hope to make on this case. At an initial meeting, letting them know that you are going to help them do some things they don't have to write a check for, but which will help avoid probate, just might carry more weight than any mention of life insurance. This doesn't mean

---

6   Primary, Contingent, Second Contingent, and For the Benefit Of (FBO) registrations (for minor beneficiaries)

7   Payable on Death designations, Transfer on Death designations, Joint w/ Payable on Second Death designations, Per Stirpes designations, Contingent designations, For the Benefit Of (FBO) designations (for accounts that may go to a minor), etc.

that life insurance won't come up at the appropriate time in the process, and when it does, following the introduction of a strategy which will provide significant additional benefits, it will happen with ease and acceptance.

Letting them know that, though you aren't licensed in the arena and can't be compensated for doing so, you are going to have an associate in the liability insurance industry perform an objective review and analysis of their homeowner's and auto liability insurance policies adds value to having you on the team. Coincidentally, that associate is going to be motivated to introduce you to his clients as well.

These preliminary concepts are acceptable considerations for someone with a "checking you out" mindset. Any discussion about financial products is only appropriate at a second or third meeting. Financial products can be introduced only after you have gathered financial data, helped your client determine personal objectives, analyzed their individual situation and financial positions, unveiled financial vulnerabilities they knew about and those they didn't know they had, and then developed and presented one or more strategies that might solve those problems.

If implemented correctly; this type of "Consideration First System" is wholly beneficial in its function, to both clients and financial advisors alike. First, this system will afford your clients a "self-actuating mindset" and confidence; that they've entrusted both their future, and their family's legacy to a financial advisor who, first and foremost considers them and their financial well-being…before any thought of any financial product exists. The value of this result to you, the financial advisor during this process, cannot be overstated!

What is strategically advantageous to you here…is who you are, from your client's perspective! While you were simply being attentive and dutiful to your prospective client's prerequisites; taking the time and making the effort to extend consideration...you were also defining the integrity of your character, and communicating the fidelity of your objectives to that client! A little time and consideration, along with a thorough fact-finding assessment of your client's characteristics and situation...and you've already begun to solidify a lasting and exclusive relationship with that client. It may seem hard to believe; but *all* of these mutually-beneficial relationship-building resources are attainable through the simplest gestures of respect and personal consideration. However, even though financial products will eventually solve the problems, this is done <u>without</u> mentioning a product during the introductory phase of a client meeting.

Somewhere along the line, we, as financial advisors, have developed the notion that trustworthiness and client service differentiate us from the rest of the herd. Nothing could be further from the truth. These are the most basic attributes of financial advisors. If you are going to differentiate yourself and your practice, you have to do something different. The reality is that there isn't anything you can offer that the other advisors in your town can't offer, **but you probably can offer something the other advisors in your city aren't offering**. If you really want to understand this dynamic, read "How to Get Your Competition Fired (Without Saying Anything Bad About Them)"[8]

With the above foundation as a backdrop, let's explore some functional ways in which an advisor can do what we have described. During a data gathering session, a client's mindset is completely comfortable with a question like, "Do you think you might be more comfortable investing for growth and accepting the fluctuations doing so is likely to bring, or would you feel better investing more conservatively, with a

---

8   By Randy Schwantz - Publisher: Wiley

goal of leveling out the fluctuations you would expect your portfolio to provide?" This question is much more likely to be well received than an advisor, who during the first meeting, is hailing the benefits of either of those ways of investing. The former is client consideration; the latter is "selling", the very thing the client was concerned might occur.

We have established that understanding a prospective client's mindset at different points in the financial planning or advisory process is critical for the comfort of the client, which leads to successful implementation for the advisor. Implementation occurs because when you do get to the input that relates to financial products, they might actually hear it. At that point, they aren't in a resistive mindset.

Recognize that personal interactions they experience before meeting you can drastically enhance or restrict your effectiveness in the planning process. Let's look at an example.

Assume you are beginning your second meeting with a new client. They have brought in all their records, statements, estate documents, etc. You enjoy some small talk and then launch into your standard data gathering process. However, what if three days prior to your meeting; your new client had a conversation with a co-worker, who had urgently warned them to beware of "financial advisors" because their brother had just been scammed by one? What if the result of that conversation was that your client walked into your office seriously considering just leaving his money in the bank?

Would it help you to know what his mindset was, before you started asking personal questions? Would it be beneficial to you and your new client if you asked at the beginning of the meeting:

1) "Do you have any new or existing concerns about anything relating to what we are about to do?"

2) "Has anything changed since we last talked?"

3) "Do you have anything that you would like to address before we begin?"

If your new client then tells you about his co-worker's conversation you might be well advised to do a time out from data gathering to explain that in your office you don't use escrow accounts like Bernie Madoff did, which gave him personal access to his clients' funds. It might be very beneficial for your client to understand that at no time do you or your staff ever have access to the monies in his accounts.

How much more *comfortable* will your client be during the data gathering process, after you successfully address this issue? How much more *focused* on the task at hand and open to constructive input will your client be during the data gathering process, after you successfully get this potential issue off the table? Would that conversation help to facilitate the continuation of the process? How much would it enhance the odds of actually implementing a financial plan? Wouldn't your time together be more effective if you identified and addressed this concern head on, leaving everyone at ease, rather than allow unknown but totally avoidable resistance to fester?

The point here is that if you ask the question(s), you will know, because they will tell you. Almost without exception, you are going to have exactly the answer to put their minds at ease. But, if you don't ask, you won't know, and you won't have the opportunity to provide that answer, to address that issue. Consider your client, and the client relationship will be considerate of you.

A fatal error in our industry is thinking that client consideration is just about making the right recommendations i.e. suggesting the appropriate investment vehicles. This just isn't the case. Client consideration means considering your clients and their current attitude and mindset from the moment you start talking to them. Client consideration is helping them ease into a comfortable and receptive attitude. Client consideration is about them, meaning where they are mentally and emotionally from the beginning. Only after their minds are at ease, can you deliver options they will want to consider and likely employ. Only then will they be capable of hearing what you are saying about solutions. ***The most basic client consideration is helping your clients transition from "What are you selling? I don't want any!" to "So, how do we make this happen?"*** These are the steps you can take to do that effectively from the beginning of the relationship.

In conclusion to the idea that Life is a Mirror, rather than say it is the case, let me just say that all belief systems are mental models. They are ideas to which we subscribe and based on which we make life decisions. This particular model has served me better than any of the ones to which I subscribed previously, and I have yet to experience a circumstance or an event which discredited it. For me, it certainly works better than "Everything and everybody else in my life is to blame for what doesn't work to my liking in my life". So, for me, it will just have to do until something better comes along.

CHAPTER SIX

Where is Your Client... Financially?

Contrary to popular belief in our industry, gathering your client's statements isn't sufficient financial data gathering. If you are going to consider your client, you must know minute details about his or her financial world that he or she never even knew existed, and that their current advisor, if any, never addressed. If your clients aren't routinely saying, "You know, no one ever asked me that before" or "No one ever mentioned that", then you may be missing the boat (say missing opportunities to build relationship more effectively and implement more often). Let's look at an example of how important this is to your client, even though they aren't aware of its existence, much less its significance. You will see that considering them benefits them, benefits you, and furthers the financial planning process.

One of the most valuable things you can provide for a client is a Balance Sheet. When clients come to you, many times they do so because they are, in their own words, disorganized. This means that they don't know:

1) Exactly what they have

2) What it is worth

3) The exact nature of the individual components of what they have

4) How the different things integrate or could, potentially, integrate with each other into a cohesive picture

5) How they can expect the things they already have to function for them at retirement time

6) Exactly what they owe

7) How their current debt level will impact their retirement picture

Helping them get organized is as simple as creating a Balance Sheet with Assets, Liabilities, and Net Worth. Current industry regulation doesn't allow you to deliver a Balance Sheet (consolidated statement you can alter) to clients without first verifying with your compliance department the values of each entry on the form, but you can use a Balance Sheet as a planning tool to assist you in communicating with your clients, developing a financial plan, creating an asset allocation model, and integrating the various elements of a financial, tax, and estate plan.

The Balance Sheet you will create comes from the statements they bring you and from your conversations with them. You will include:

1) Bank and credit union Checking Accounts

2) Bank and credit union Savings Accounts

3) Bank and credit union Money Market Accounts

4) Internet Savings Accounts

5) Brokerage Money Market Accounts

6) Bank and credit union Certificates of Deposit.

7) Life Insurance Cash Values

8) US Savings Bonds

9) Brokerage Security Accounts

10) Annuities

11) Mutual Funds

12) Managed Accounts

13) Limited Partnerships

14) Real Estate Investment Trusts

15) Business Development Companies

16) IRA's

17) Roth IRA's

18) Inherited IRA's

19) 403(b)'s

20) 401(k)'s

21) Roth 401(k)'s

22) Deferred Compensation (457) Plans

23) Lump Sum Pension Accounts

24) Employee Stock Option Plans

25) Employee Stock Purchase Plans

26) Personal Property - Furniture, appliances, automobiles, jewelry, art, collectibles, sporting equipment, etc. (yard sale prices)

27) Residence

28) Second Residence

29) Vacation Homes

30) Rental Property

31) Other Real Estate

32) Time Share Condos

33) Coin Collections

34) Other (any other assets they own)

35) Liabilities

For each of these assets, you will want to include the name of the institution where the asset is housed, and the name(s) on the account. Additionally, you will want to list the disclosed value of each of these assets. See Exhibit A – Balance Sheet below.

We found that we were not willing to incur the cost of forwarding to our compliance department written verification for each source of account values, so we do not deliver Balance Sheets to clients. However, we found that we could provide them a reasonable alternative with eMoney©[9]. Account balances are updated numerous times during the day, clients can access it from a computer anywhere, and they can print their own copies. eMoney sites have the ability to provide updated values on all of their financial accounts and liabilities and we are not in the "verification" business.

---

9   www.emoneyadvisor.com

Exhibit A – Balance Sheet:

Name(s)
Balance Sheet as of:

Assets	Registration		Value
Cash & Cash Equivalents			
Checking: Bank	Joint		0.00
Checking: Credit Union	Joint - POD		0.00
Savings: Bank	Joint		0.00
CD: Credit Union	Trust		0.00
Life Ins Cash Value: Life	Name		0.00
		Subtotal:	**$0.00**
Non-Qualified			
Brokerage:	Name		0.00
Mutual Fund:	Joint - TOD		0.00
Fixed Annuity:	Name		0.00
Variable Annuity:	Name		0.00
		Subtotal:	**$0.00**
Qualified & Non-Liquid			
Residence	Joint		0.00
Personal Property	Joint		0.00
Rental:	Joint		0.00
401(k):	Name		0.00
IRA:	Name		0.00
Time Share Condo:	Name		0.00
		Subtotal:	0.00
		Total Assets:	**$0.00**
Liabilities	Rate		
Mortgage: Residence	0.00%		0.00
HELOC:	0.00%		0.00
Auto Note:	0.00%		0.00
VISA:	0.00%		0.00
		Total Liabilities:	**$0.00**

Total Assets:	$0.00
Total Liabilities:	0.00
Net Worth:	$0.00

Insured Benefits:	Invested	W/D's	Value	G'ntd Min Death Benefit	Gnt'd Min W/D Base	Gnt'd An W/D Amt
	0.00	0.00	0.00	0.00	0.00	0.00
	0.00	0.00	0.00	0.00	0.00	0.00
	0.00	0.00	0.00	0.00	0.00	0.00

For planning purposes - Not to be delivered to clients without verification of values through compliance department

While the Balance Sheet is a good start, it isn't the sum total of the information you need to provide your new client along with appropriate input as to potential adjustments / improvements. Many advisors in our industry use some form of the "Bucket Approach" to asset allocation. Some use a "Now Money", "Soon Money", and "Later Money" approach. Adding the following more sophisticated, but still simple categorization will help your new clients move monumental steps toward reallocation based on objectives. Equally importantly, it helps them do so while you are gathering data, long before you ever get to the point of making suggestions for improvements. This often eliminates any need for selling, closing, overcoming objections, etc., all of which helps your client make improvements easily without objection or resistance.

Simply adding the following spreadsheet to your data gathering process helps your client understand where they are now as to asset allocation and why they might want to make adjustments without the need for "selling". See Exhibit B – Categorization Spreadsheet.

See Exhibit B – Categorization Spreadsheet*

Exhibit B

Asset Categorization

Checking	Reserve	Fallback	Insr'd Inc	Alts	Stk Mkt	Legacy	Total*
2,300.00	10,000.00	60,000.00	400,000.00	100,000.00	340,000.00	100,000.00	1,000,000.00
		6.00%	40.00%	10.00%	34.00%	10.00%	100.00%

The column heading is the asset category.

The second line is the total value of all assets in that category.

The third line is the percentage of the Total for which that category accounts.

All of this is easily set up using an Excel spreadsheet with calculation formulas.

* Total includes investment accounts only i.e. does not include Checking or Reserve

1) Checking – Self defined

2) Reserve – Your client's savings and money market accounts and CD's

3) Fallback – What they fall back on if they run out of money in the bank: Mutual Funds w/ conservative equity income, short term bonds, and floating rate funds[10]

4) Insured Income - Annuities[11]

5) Alternatives[12] - Higher risk, non-liquid, expected better performance

6) Managed Market[13] - Securities based on client's risk tolerance parameters

7) Legacy – Life insurance cash values. Legacy planning is not estate planning. Estate planning is designed to eliminate probate and prevent unintended heirs. Legacy planning is used when clients have funds they don't expect to need for personal income, are willing to take these funds off the "income" table, and wish to provide an insured, tax free, no probate benefit to heirs that is higher than the amount they allocate to this category. Generally, and when clients qualify for same, last to die life insurance is used here.

Assume that you discover in the early data gathering process (you have a statement already in hand) that your new client owns an annuity. While the statement has the standard account information such as Issue Date, Invested Amount, Account Value, and Rider Benefits, there is still additional, critical information that the statement is

---

10   At time of publication author found bank savings accounts paying .2%
11   Insured benefits subject to the claim paying ability of the insuring carrier
12   Uninsured, higher risk, and no assurance of performance
13   Uninsured; value will fluctuate with stock and bond market fluctuations; shares liquidated while market values are less than the price paid will result in capital loss. Past performance is no assurance of future performance.

lacking. One of the most considerate things you can do for your client is to find out what that missing information is, and then help them to understand what it means. With the client at your desk to authorize the process, if you will call their company and ask all of the questions needed to fully complete Exhibit C – Annuity Analysis (below), you will have critical information that your client never considered. This information will lead directly to your delivered options for improvement, not because of your selling ability, but because of you revealing gaps, unsubstantiated costs, unnecessary risks, etc. This information will help you know specifically whether your client can take steps to improve that contract either through restructuring or replacement, and the service rep at their existing company will oftentimes deliver and confirm this information for your client on the speaker phone at your desk. It will also confirm if this account should be maintained because of surrender penalties, insured benefits greater than account values, or other factors.

If you are a current licensed advisor; everything on the client's account statement will probably be familiar to you, and potentially to your client as well. However; my advice to you to here is... ***become educated beyond the obvious, be meticulous in your data gathering. Don't assume that because of what you do know that you know all that matters. Don't underestimate the value of a complete client profile.*** As you will next see, there is one area in particular that has a startling potential for beneficiary misfortune, if left haphazardly, though inadvertently, overlooked. The following pages will not only showcase a situational example from which this type of financial tragedy may occur, but they will provide an additional opportunity for an advisor to significantly differentiate himself from his new prospective client's current advisor, never having said a bad word about that advisor.

Extending your clients the consideration they so richly deserve is a simple task to perform - when you've taken the time and effort to equip yourself with the educational resources that enable you to shed some light on looming areas of financial concern. Before we look at the specific problem to which I am referring, let me tell you a story about how one simple issue, and knowledge as to how to remove it, helped me obtain a client where there was "no possible way he was going to change financial advisors!"

I met Larry and Christine at an educational program I taught at a retirement community in Jacksonville. He was a retired Army general and he and his wife had moved to Florida from Wisconsin. The program I taught and that they had attended was called, "Who Really Gets Your Stuff" and focused on the pitfalls in traditional estate planning efforts.

When Larry and Christine came to see me, he explained that he wanted to talk to me about fine-tuning his estate plan because of some concerns he already had and some unknown ones my presentation had raised. He warned me early on that there was no possibility, however, that he would ever change financial advisors. He went on to explain that his advisor, still back in Wisconsin, was a young lady of whom he and Christine were quite fond. She came to Florida once a year and met with them and when she did she stayed at their residence with them. They went to dinner together; they socialized; he was somewhat of a mentor for her, not as to financial matters, but personally. It seemed she had dated some unsavory character, and Larry had convinced her of the wisdom of severing the relationship. She took his advice and was the better off for having done so!

When I heard this, I knew there wasn't a sales pitch in the world that was going to sway Larry in another direction… and I told him so. I explained that I did not take clients exclusively for estate planning work without reviewing everything they were doing financially. But, I explained, once everything was addressed, what he did or didn't do was up to him and he was free to implement or not implement any of the options I presented.

I then shared with Larry and Christine that, if they elected to engage us, and if we accepted them as clients, we were going to go through a process. I then looked across the desk at Larry and told him that at some point in that process he was going to have to make a decision between

1) The value of the relationship between them and their existing advisor, and…

2) What was best financially for him, for Christine, for their children, and for their grandchildren.

I told Larry that he would know when that point came and that I was not going to ask them to change advisors; in fact, I wasn't going to mention the subject again; when that point came, it would be up to him to bring it up. He reiterated again, quite emphatically, that he would never change financial advisors. (Reiterated again is from the "Department of Redundancy Department"!)

Half way through our next meeting, Larry looked at Christine and said, "We have to do this!" and we began the process of transferring all of their assets to accounts at Gold Tree Financial. At this point, we had not discussed any of the financial vehicles I would later disclose as options in his Asset Allocation Model. We had not compared rates of returns between his existing portfolio and our track record. We hadn't yet addressed the costs and/or tax liability to liquidating or repositioning assets.

What follows is what caused Larry to make that 180 degree

turnaround - during the data gathering process - with no selling, no closing, no power phrases designed to overcome objections, and, in fact, without me even asking for his business. As a consideration for our clients, we do an analysis of everything they currently have. For annuities, this analysis includes completing the below spreadsheet that allows us to determine all of the relevant parameters of their existing annuities. Please note carefully the items included in this analysis spreadsheet. See Exhibit C – Annuity Analysis.

Exhibit C – Annuity Analysis:

Existing Annuity Analysis

Home Phone:	0	Today's Date	Analysis Date
First	0		
First	0		

Existing Annuities:			
Owner			
Company			
Phone Number			
Product Name			
Annuity Type			
Tax Status			
Cost Basis			
Account Number			
Issue Date			
Maturity Date			
Is Maturity Date a Forced Annuitization Date?			
Invested Amount			
Bonus %			
Bonus Amount			
Withdrawals			
Current Account Value			
Allocation or Crediting Method			
Crediting Cap, if Applicable			
Surrender Charge Percentage			
Surrender Charge Amount			
MVA Adjustment			
Benefit Charge			
Surrender Value			
-0- Surrender Penalty Date			
Guaranteed Living Benefits:			
Gntd W/D Base Calculation	*1	*4	*7
Gntd W/D Base Amount			
Gntd W/D An Amount			
Next Auto Step-Up Date			
Guaranteed Death Benefit Calc.	*2	*5	*8
Guaranteed Death Benefit Amt*			
Systematic RMD's (Y / N / n/a)			
Additional Information...	*3	*6	*9
Beneficiaries:			
Primary			
Contingent			

The below section provides you enough space to include verbiage on specific benefit details...

*1

*2

*3

Etc...

Now, look specifically at the following two items:

Maturity Date

Forced Annuitization Date

Every annuity has a maturity date. What most clients don't know is that many annuities have a Forced Annuitization clause which triggers on Maturity Date. This simply means that the company will automatically, or with notice without client response, annuitize the contract and initiate annuity payments. Annuitization can be a very beneficial part of a well-designed financial plan, but it can also quickly become a catastrophic event if left undirected.

To structure this example - Let's assume that the clients are a happily married couple named Fred and Wilma. A quick note - In the interest of conserving time; and directly retrieving the core value from the information being presented, the details of our couple's timeline have been condensed. Looking for safety related to their financial future, Fred decides to purchase an annuity. Let's assume that his contract will reach its Maturity Date when the contract owner reaches age ninety. Further, for the purposes of quantifying this example, let's assume that the initial investment paid into the contract was $100,000.

Now let's jump forward in time to present day: Twenty years and Fred have now passed; Wilma has inherited his contract and is now the owner. That initial $100,000 policy is now worth $324,618. Assume that when the Maturity Date of the contract comes, the insuring company mails the elderly Wilma a letter of notification, advising her that the Maturity Age had been reached, and that payments from the contract must begin.

In the scenario above – When the letter reaches Wilma, she may open it and she may not. It could wind up behind the dresser or in a stack of other unopened mail. If this happens and she doesn't respond, the automatic default provision will be triggered, the "Life Only Annuitization" provision. Therefore; in accordance with company protocol, Wilma will be automatically issued her first annuity check.

Offering an alternative to the previous scenario: what if Wilma receives, opens, and reads the notification letter; but doesn't have a clue what they are talking about? They provide her options, but again, no need to worry…"No action is required" said the letter, and once again, the company will initiate its provisional "Life Only Annuitization".

Sadly, if Wilma receives her first check and then dies four months later, the company owes her remaining heirs nothing. "By default" in not responding to the letter; Wilma agreed to the terms of the contract, which said annuitization would occur. Dear old Wilma has unknowingly just disinherited her children, grandchildren, and any other intended heirs, effectively naming the insurance company as her only beneficiary! While annuitization is a valuable and reasonable alternative at certain ages, in certain situations, it isn't likely to be a good move for Wilma and her family for her to annuitize at age ninety!

It should be noted: nothing was malicious, illegal, or untoward on the part of the insurance company or the advisor who wrote the contract for Fred in this situation. As advisors, we know that an annuitization that is structured the right way, within the right financial plan, can prove greatly beneficial to our clients. However; as in the situation described above, an automatic annuitization by default, could quickly become financially devastating to its intended beneficiaries if they are not informed!

As to Larry and Christine; I had Larry's insurance company service rep on the speaker phone in my office with Larry and Christine sitting at my desk. They had authorized the service rep to answer some questions I had and I completed the spreadsheet in front of them. The service rep confirmed that with their company (a major well respected insurer) when Maturity Date comes, without instructions to the contrary, **annuitization is automatic.** Once Larry understood this, the emotional response was significant. Sitting at my desk, his comment was, "Hal, how could my advisor let this be the case? She is a professional. Why would she not tell us this and why would we not have this x-dated in our calendar so we would be sure to head it off?" This was the moment when he turned to Christine and said, "We have to do this!"

I gently explained to Larry and Christine that there was nothing intentional in this. First of all, many of us won't live to age ninety. Secondly, his advisor was likely completely unaware of the potential for, in his case, $400,000 plus dollars to be inherited by his insurance company. Thirdly, annuities are designed to annuitize. It is incumbent on the owner of the annuity; or someone on their team who is able to address such potential issues, to know exactly what they own, and to make sure their desired objectives for themselves and their families are accomplished.

In a single act of exceptional client consideration; an advisor can help a client prevent a major disinheriting of intended heirs, and raise his or her own stock in the minds and hearts of that client, in a way that no sales pitch in the world could ever hope to accomplish. Suddenly, on the spot, the client just gets it…they understand that they have now graduated from a sales agent, to a financial planner or advisor who is both considerate and experienced, knowledgeable and proactive. In this pivotal moment, the value of this newly reached understanding is immeasurable. We went from prospective client and "I am never going to change financial advisors!" to "We have to do this" without ever once asking for the order. Once realized; the likelihood of implementation following one of these conversations can rise exponentially, possibly becoming absolute! Next, you will suggest improvements, and show them how to fix the problem, a consummate act of client consideration, for which you will be compensated. In the process, you get all of their other accounts and a lifetime relationship in which you will use other ideas contained herein to make their financial lives better.

The exact same thing can happen in relation to life insurance. Prospective clients are often "on guard" for "insurance based" practices. I have heard it many times, "That guy just wanted to sell me life insurance!" Yet improvements in your client's financial world often include adding life insurance; or replacing their existing life insurance policies that have aged, as outdated policies often times prove more costly to the client.

If my new clients own existing life insurance policies, we move to the "Life Insurance Analysis". See Exhibit D – Life Insurance Analysis. This analysis is to life insurance what the Annuity Analysis is to annuities. This process gives us a complete x-ray of all of their existing insurance policies, which reveals inadequacies, overlaps, and cost/value mismatches. Ferreting out these issues conveys professionalism, evidences careful due-diligence, and signals a clear personal commitment to client consideration.

Exhibit D – Life Insurance Analysis:

6/16/2015	Last	First	First
1/0/1900	Insurable:	No	Yes
	Date of Birth		
	Age	#VALUE!	#VALUE!

Home Phone	0
First	0
First	0

Create a spreadsheet with the following collumn headings and cells for values for each:

Insured	Company	Phone	Policy Number	Policy Date	Type	Face Value	Paid Up Additions

Policy Loan	Dividends @ Interest	Net Death Benefit	Gross Cash Value	Surrender Charge	Net Cash Value and Dividends @ Interest	Net Insurance	Annual Premium

Annual Loan Int	Last Annual Dividend	Last Annual Cost	Premium Increase Date	Renewal Premium	Projected Termination Date	Convertibility Expiration Date	Primary Beneficiary

Contingent Beneficiary

At the bottom of your spreadsheet include these notes:

Options:
1) Keep - If you need or want life insurance coverage, and, either...
   A. You aren't insurable, or...
   B. You can't improve on the cost / value parameters of the existing policy
2) Cancel or Sell - If you don't need or want the overage
3) Replace - If you want or need life insurance coverage, and...
   A. You are insurable, and...
   B. You can improve on the cost / value parameters of the existing policy

Reasons to replace a life insurance policy:
1) Coverage stays in force longer with the new policy, or...
2) The new policy gives you more coverage for the same premium, or...
3) The new policy gives you the same coverage for less premium

Before lapsing any policy that isn't being rolled over to another
life insurance policy or annuity, obtain cost basis / tax liability
including consideration for loans and dividends received.

We never recommend cancelling a life insurance policy. If it is
in your best financial interest to cancel an existing policy,
you will decide that based on your personal objectives.

Place column headings shown all on one line across an Excel spreadsheet

Again, with your client at your desk, if you will call existing insurance companies and obtain a thorough report on all existing life insurance policies, you will have concrete basis for comparing existing and available life insurance protection. Only by knowing exactly what they have, can you make an accurate determination of appropriate next steps.

Little things can be extremely helpful and relevant. Where clients, individually, or jointly, are not still insurable, knowing existing cash value amounts and elected dividend options can provide the basis for substantially more life insurance without additional cost. This may be doable by simply changing dividend disposition elections. Where clients are still insurable, consolidating policies may substantially increase coverage, or reduce cost for the same coverage. (Providing your clients with both options means that you are taking care of them, not just trying to make a sale.) But you wouldn't have known of the opportunity for doing either without complete detailed information on existing coverages! Following this exercise, oftentimes, no sales pitch is needed when writing a substantial life insurance policy is the appropriate next step, and what a beautiful and considerate thing to do for your clients.

The best method for assembling an accurate comparative analysis of your client's data is to – actually gather all of their data…yourself! Writing a new policy isn't always the solution you are seeking. Adjusting the "Dividend Options" on an existing policy, resulting in an increasing death benefit, or lower premiums for life, provides great value to your new client, and solidifies the case for other improvements on which you will be compensated.

Uncovering the fact that their current Universal Life Insurance policy; unbeknownst to them, is slated to lapse in the future, can save clients tens or hundreds of thousands of dollars in life insurance protection they were likely to lose down the road, and in each of these cases, nothing more than a detailed analysis and a simple comparison of options is needed (See **Exhibit E(1), E(2), and E(3).** These Illustration Request Forms will provide valuable information not included in simple policy illustrations. Extending these exceptionally considerate actions to your client, sharply contrasts their previous advisor's lack of any action in this area, and they will soon conclude for themselves - they need to graduate to your services. You will find that this will start to happen automatically, without you asking. When you do things their existing (say previous) advisor never did for them, you don't have to point out the value of you and your services. It becomes obvious, all without sales pitches.

Take a close look at the last two items on Exhibit D. You will often find that clients or their agents have failed to include First Contingent and Second Contingent Beneficiary Designations on their existing life insurance policies. Correcting this assures that life insurance proceeds will pass to "intended heirs". Additionally, missing beneficiary designations generally cause policies to "default" to the estate. This causes the insurance proceeds to be forced into probate, adding substantial unnecessary cost and delay to the settlement process.

Proactively discovering and protecting your clients' families from this is most considerate on your part! Your clients' reaction will likely be, "No one ever asked me this before!", and their existing life insurance agent's stock just went down immeasurably... without you saying anything bad about him / her.

Exhibit E (1) – Universal Life Insurance Illustration Request

April 14, 2015

American General Life Insurance Company

Policyholder Service Department   Fax: (713) 831-3028

Re: Policy # _____

Gentlemen,

Please provide <u>the following information</u> on the above referenced policies, each. **Please run all illustrations to Age 100**.

1) As is, with <u>current</u> interest rates, mortality charges, and premiums, at what age is policy projected to lapse?   Age _____

<u>and</u>...

2) If "as is" illustration at current rates and charges <u>runs out</u> before age 100... What is the minimum premium required to have $1,000 in cash value at age 100?   Premium _____

<u>or...</u>

If "as is" illustration <u>does not run out</u> before age 100 ...

1) At current rates and charges, to what amount could we reduce the premium between now and age 100 to still have $1,000 in cash value at age 100?   Premium _____

<u>and</u>...

2) At current rates and charges, if we keep paying the current premium, at what age could we stop paying premiums and still have $1,000 in cash value at age 100. Age _____

Also:

What is the current Maturity Age of the policy?   Age _____

Can Maturity Age be extended? Yes _____ No _____ If yes, to what age? Age _____

Is there an age at which, if the policy is still in force, there are no further costs associated w/ the policy?   Yes _____ No _____ If yes, at what age? Age _____

Please e-mail illustrations or answers to the above questions to (your email address).

With all answers, illustrations are not required.

For answers, please copy this request form and complete separately for each policy.

Respectfully,

(Client Name)
(Client Address)
(Client City, State Zip)
(Client Phone Number)

Exhibit E (2) VUL Illustration Request

April 14, 2015

AXA Equitable

Policyholder Service Department   Fax No: (810) 632-6745

Re: Policy #   157201295

Gentlemen,

Please provide me <u>a copy of a current statement</u> and <u>the following information</u> on the above referenced policy. **Please run all illustrations to Age 100**.

3) Assuming zero and 6% rates of return, respectively, on policy invested cash values, at <u>current</u> mortality charges and premiums, at what age is this policy projected to lapse?

At 0%   Lapse at Age _____

At 6%   Lapse at Age _____

<u>and</u>...

4) If "as is" illustration at 0% above <u>runs out</u> before age 100, at 0% what is the minimum premium required to have $1,000 in cash value at age 100?   Premium _____

<u>or</u>...

If "as is" illustration at 0% <u>does not run out</u> before age 100 …

3) At above rates and charges, to what amount could we reduce the premium between now and age 100 to at 0% still have $1,000 in cash value at age 100?   Premium _____

<u>and</u>…

4) At 0% rate and current charges, if we keep paying the current premium, at 0% at what age could we stop paying premiums and still have $1,000 in cash value at age 100?

Age _____

<u>Also:</u>

What is the current Maturity Age of the policy?   Age _____

Can Maturity Age be extended? Yes ____ No____ If yes, to what age? Age ____

Is there an age at which, if the policy is still in force, there are no further costs associated w/ the policy?   Yes _____ No _____ If yes, at what age?   Age____

Please e-mail illustrations and all information to (<u>your email address</u>), or just e-mail the answers to the above questions. With all answers, illustrations are not required.

Respectfully,

(Client Name)
(Client Address)
(Client City, State Zip)
(Client Phone Number)

Exhibit E (3) WL Illustration Request

April 14, 2015

New York Life Insurance

51 Madison Avenue

New York, NY 10010

Policyholder Service Department   Fax Number: (216) 227-6625

Re: Policy #:   43 284 794

Gentlemen,

Please provide <u>the following information</u> on the above referenced policy.

1) By contract, I have several Dividend Options. On my policy, which Dividend Option am I utilizing?

   A. Dividend check to owner   _____

   B. Dividends applying toward premium   _____

   C. Dividends buying Paid Up Additions   _____

   D. Dividends buying Paid Up Additions and Surrendering Paid Up Additions to apply toward premium   _____

   E. Dividends accumulating at interest   _____

   F. Other: _____   _____

2) Assuming current dividend rate (which I understand is not guaranteed) to what age will the policy continue if I pay no more premiums?

> Projected   Age _____
>
> Guaranteed Age _____

3) Is my current Dividend Option choice resulting in a systematic change in Death Benefit Amount? _____ Is this change, if any, positive or negative? _____

4) If there is a change, and it is negative, how much premium would I need to pay annually at projected Dividend Rates in order to keep the death benefit level? Premium Amount $_____

5) Is this policy scheduled to Endow in the future?
Yes _____ No _____ If so, Age _____

Please e-mail answers to the above questions to (Your email address). With all answers, illustrations are not required. For answers, please copy this request form and fill in the blanks.

Please note that simply providing an Illustration of Values will not answer the above questions.

Your assistance is appreciated.

Respectfully,

(Client Name)
(Client Address)
(Client City, State Zip)
(Client Phone Number)

This introduces an opportunity to comment on one of the items listed in the next chapter. When verbalizing client's options, always leave the first option as the option to do nothing, to leave things as they are. This eliminates the potential for a perception that you're trying to push them into some action of your choosing. Pushing triggers resistance, the very mindset you don't want to manifest. Clients spell "pushing" s-e-l-l-i-n-g. Reminding them that their first option is to do nothing...to leave things as they already are, shows your clients that you are planning, not selling. Clients are most pleasantly disposed to entertaining creative strategies...they go out of their way to avoid sales pitches and sales people.

CHAPTER SEVEN

42 Specific Things You Can Do That Are Considerate of Your Clients

Below, I am going to provide a summarized list of forty two things that you can implement within your practice to afford your clients the highest element of consideration, while differentiating yourself from others who think they are your competition. Some of these things have already been referenced above, but having a checklist as you progress may prove helpful. Additionally; this could also be solid content for discussion at your next staff meeting. Distribute the checklist to other team members, add to it, and ask them to add to it. Getting everyone in your office focused on client consideration will unify your goals as a practice, and will serve to enhance the relationships between your staff members and potential and existing clients. Remember, the purpose of all this is to make your practice a "client based" practice. The road runs through client consideration.

1) First thing, ask your first time visit prospective client why they would sit down at the desk of a financial advisor / planner and listen to what they tell you. Whether they tell you why, so you will know what they are looking for, or tell you that they aren't sure if they even need to be there, each is a critical bit of information for you to consider in the ensuing meeting!

2) Before you tell them anything about yourself or your practice, ask if they have any particular questions they would like to ask or areas they would like to address. This gives them the opening to discuss what is prominent in their minds, if anything.

3) Tell your perspective clients why you do what you do the way you do it. (In order to do this, you must first determine this for yourself, about yourself. Read "Start With Why"*, but before telling them why, ask them why – see 1) above. This allows you to share with your prospective client who you are in relation to your practice.

4) If you are tied up for even *one minute* after the time for your client's scheduled appointment, make sure someone on your staff is sitting in your office waiting area with them and talking to them while they are waiting for you.

5) If you are late for your appointment (again, even by one minute) as you escort your clients into your office, apologize for keeping them waiting. (Remember how unconsidered you felt last time you waited over an hour to see your doctor?)

6) When your staff serves drinks or snacks, have them do so

---

*   by Simon Sinek: Penguin Group

always using a nice serving tray. This may seem like window dressing, but it elicits a definite emotional reaction. You will witness this through the comments they make about the tray.

7) Have your staff record "Client Preferences" in your computer so the next time Nancy comes in your assistant "remembers" that she likes "two sugars and one cream" in her coffee. As part of this procedure, have your staff **also record** in your computer any **food allergies, sensitivities, or intolerances** if/when they are already known, openly disclosed, or when substitutions and/or alternatives are requested by your clients. (Common Concerns: Peanuts/Peanut Butter, Milk/Dairy, Gluten/Wheat)

8) Never discuss any financial product in the first meeting — never, ever, no matter what. This is a hard and fast rule; never break it! There are no exceptions, even if the client brings it up, asks you specifically, or requests information about a specific financial product.

9) Anticipate and expect first time visitor concerns, uncertainties, and intentional cautiousness. Assume that they are just afraid rather than that they are being difficult, and consciously shift your approach with them toward a gentle-mannered demeanor!

10) If you don't have a sense of "where" your clients are mentally or emotionally, ask them. A good question to ask is "What did you talk about on the way over this morning that you wouldn't say in front of me?"

11) Tell your prospective clients that they can't buy anything, write any checks, make any changes, or sign up for anything today. Let them know you are both here just to determine whether a relationship with each other would be beneficial.

12) Never give prospective clients data forms to complete at home or alone; instead, give them a checklist of items to bring in to you. See Exhibit F – List of Items Needed for Financial, Tax, & Estate Planning. This completely eliminates potential resistance to completing forms. It eliminates the laborious task of transferring information from their statements to the data form, prevents errors on their part, and insures that you gather accurate information. Maybe most importantly, this also prevents you from losing a small percentage of your prospective clients who never got around to completing the data questionnaire (but never admitted to you that was why they didn't come back).

13) After asking about objectives and gathering the data, spend some time just talking with your client(s). Mostly, ask questions and listen to what they tell you.

14) Tell prospective clients a little about yourself. Be willing to reveal who you are outside of your office. Share with them, the person you really are. Then ask, listen, and learn about the people your clients really are from the information, and stories they'll share with you.

15) Promise your clients they will never get a sales pitch at your desk.

16) Keep your promise!

17) In every instance, define the problem before you offer a solution. (A solution without a problem is a sales pitch. More importantly, a solution without a client's perception of a problem is a sales pitch.)

18) Throw out all your "sales ideas" and replace them with "strategies". Many of the sales ideas you have heard about had strategies buried within them – find them and talk about them. Clients love strategies! Promise them strategies.

19) Keep your promise – Deliver strategies.

20) Instead of making recommendations, provide options. The only exception to this rule is in a "slam-dunk" situation. Slam-dunk is not defined as 'you know they will buy' — it is 'your recommendation can only result in improvement'. This obviously doesn't fit any investment with risk or which requires market performance to accomplish its objectives! It does fit custom designed account registrations and beneficiary designations.

21) When clients ask, "What would you do?" the answer is, "It isn't relevant." Tell them, "This isn't my money. It is your money. If you lose it, I've already been compensated for making it available to you. Therefore, it has to be your call. Remember: I promised you that you would never get a sales pitch at my desk."

22) Explain that you think it makes sense that:

  a. No one but them should ever decide how much risk they take – it is their money

  b. You decide jointly how much money should go into each Asset Allocation category – You understand the allocation system / they know what their objectives are

  c. You pick the vehicles – You do the research and have the expertise to know the difference between them

  d. Having said all that, how they actually do it is their call!

23) In every instance, remind your clients that the first option is to "Leave things as they are."

24) Explain in the simplest terms; how your planning process works, and then stay true to the process.

25) Never have a conversation with a staff member that you wouldn't have in front of a client.

26) Train your staff members to never have a conversation with each other that they wouldn't have in front of a client.

27) Never make a note in your computer you wouldn't want your client to read.

28) Never put your client in the "hot seat" by asking them to make a decision to buy, playing a game of "the first one to speak loses" (Marketing 101). Instead, unveil a plan that has a better chance of accomplishing their objectives than their current one, and then walk them into your assistant's office to do the paperwork.

29) Never demean your clients' old advisor. Show them what has been missed, and help them "graduate" to what you do that is better.

30) Directly address your client's relationship with their old advisor and help them get past it.. (See Chapter Eight - Helping your clients fire a former advisor)

31) Stay in touch with your clients. A weekly newsletter does this nicely. Platinum Advisor Marketing provides a great copy ready version with Stock Market Update and Economic Commentary (even if I do wish they would take "marketing" out of their name.)[15]

---

15   Platinum Advisor Marketing - http://www.platinumadvisormarketing.com/

32) Once your prospective client becomes your client, ask her why she did, and listen to what she tells you.

33) Do annual reviews.

34) Control what you can control.

35) Acknowledge what you can't control and make certain your client understands the difference. Clients would like to assume we will make certain they don't lose money and, if they invest in marketable securities, we have no ability to do that.

36) Do something for your clients after they invest with you. A monthly social or wine tasting in your office shows consideration and appreciation. Clients may bring their friends and you could get new clients. (It is OK if considering your clients benefits you!) We have implemented a whole "Beyond Financial" program in our office which includes monthly socials and educational programs.

37) Never talk business at socials. If a guest asks how your practice works, the answer is, "Bill, I am drinking wine tonight. Give me your business card and I will call you tomorrow". (Prospective clients always come expecting someone to pounce at some point; they are pleasantly surprised when it doesn't happen, so there are no negatives to following up the next day with a phone call.)

38) Do a "Client Financial Organizer Workshop at your office once a month. The whole program only takes an hour and helps clients learn what to keep and what to pitch, what to store for their children's benefit to simplify the transition in case of your client's death. You can find wonderful handouts on the Internet.

39) Do a "New Client Orientation" event at your office once a month. Obviously, invite new clients, but also invite existing clients. Put together a list of things it would help them to know, like what they can expect from you, what they can't expect from you, and how to get the most value from the services you offer, etc. Ask your staff what has gone wrong in the past that wouldn't have if clients had known ahead of time. Ask your staff what have been the repeat issues they have dealt with that could have been avoided. Ask your staff what things have been issues only because of something simple your clients didn't know or understand about how your processes work after they become clients. Address these things in the event.

40) Look for opportunities to "Surprise and Delight" your best clients. Check out what Matt Oechsli[16] (Oxley) has to say on this. I've found his information to be very valuable for ways to find and engage higher net worth clients. Furthermore, his entire curriculum revolves around client consideration.

41) At the end of every prospective client and client meeting, give your clients a "Lindt Lindor Truffle". (Buy them at the department store following holidays – holiday packaged products are sold at a discount.)

42) Send your clients a birthday card with a $1.00 bill in it. It elicits exactly the same emotion it did when they were six years old. (My wife, Sandy, thought this one up and the client response has been phenomenal! Sandy came up with the idea, my assistant sends the cards, and my clients give me all the credit!)

---

16   The Oechsli Institute: *www.oechsli.com/*

Exhibit F – List of Items Needed for Financial, Tax, & Estate Planning:

Items Needed for Planning

Compile items on the list and bring to our next meeting
Please omit only items not part of your picture.

_____	____ / ____ / _____
Full Name	Date of Birth
_____	____ / ____ / _____
Full Name	Date of Birth

_____ Copy of Drivers Licenses, each (we will copy at our office if convenient)
_____ Account Statements – **Mailed copy preferred (if digital copy, include title page and asset allocations)**

_____ Checking	_____ Savings	_____ Money Market
_____ IRA's	_____ 401(k)'s _____ TSA's	_____ Deferred Comp Plans
_____ Education Plans	_____ 529's _____ Coverdell ESA's	_____ UGMA/UTMA Accounts
_____ Profit Sharing Account(s)	_____ Stock Option Plan(s)	_____ Pension(s)
_____ Mutual Fund(s)	_____ Annuities	_____ CD's
_____ Life Insurance – Cash value, premiums, dividends		_____ Brokerage Account(s)
_____ Universal, Indexed, or Variable Life Insurance Policy Annual Reports		_____ Other

_____ Social Security Benefit Statement, if currently available (not applicable at younger ages)
_____ List of stocks/bonds held in certificate form (not in a brokerage account)
_____ Most recently completed Federal Income Tax Return
_____ Copy of most recent employment pay stub
_____ Declarations Pages – Homeowners, Auto, Umbrella Insurance (Coverage, premiums, etc.)
_____ Pension Benefit Information, each; current or projected
_____ A link to the Summary Plan Description for your 401(k). (Call your Human Resource Dept.)
_____ Estate Plan Documents – wills, trusts, powers-of-attorney, etc.
_____ Debts List – Balance, interest rate, and payments
_____ Mortgages – Balance, interest rate, and payment amount (principal and interest only)
_____ Real Estate List – Name, approximate fair market value
_____ An existing beneficiary designation form from a life insurance policy, annuity, IRA, or retirement plan
_____ Company Benefits (healthcare, group life insurance, long-term disability insurance, etc)
_____ Notes on anything else you think might be relevant to your financial situation
$_____ Personal Property Value – Furniture, appliances, jewelry, collectibles, vehicles, etc. (Not an itemized list, just a total; use yard sale prices, not replacement or insured value)

If you have trouble finding anything on the list, don't delay your next appointment trying to find it! We will follow-up on additional items later.

Scott Showers, CFP®, Harold J. Rogers, CFP®, Ryan M. Newton, CFP® and Ashish Bajaj: Advisory services offered through Investment Advisors, a division of ProEquities, Inc., a Registered Investment Advisor. Securities offered through ProEquities, Inc., a Registered Broker-Dealer, Member, FINRA & SIPC. Sue Walker and Ashish Bajaj are Registered Representatives of ProEquities, Inc. Gold Tree Financial (GTF), Inc. is independent of ProEquities, Inc.

Scott Showers	scott@gtfjax.com	8596 Arlington Expressway	Phone:	904 725-0556
Harold J. Rogers, CFP®	hal@gtfjax.com	Jacksonville, FL 32211	Toll-Free:	888 720-0556
Ryan M. Newton, CFP®	ryan@gtfjax.com		Fax:	904 720-1909
Sue P. Walker, FLMI	sue@gtfjax.com			
Ashish K. Bajaj	ashish@gtfjax.com			

CHAPTER EIGHT

Consummate Acts of Client Consideration

Three consummate acts of client consideration deserve more attention:

1) Specifically helping prospective clients feel safe with you

2) Helping clients fire their former advisor

3) Increasing the chances that prospective clients will get past the initial interview

Making prospective clients feel 'safe' with you

Every new prospective client who walks into your office will likely have some fears and reservations as they consider a relationship with a financial advisor they don't know. Addressing those reservations during the first meetings, and consciously laying them to rest, is an act of consideration toward your clients.

As we have already discussed, the immediate concern that must be overcome if subsequent meetings are to take place at all is the concern that someone is going to try to sell them something. Recognize that this concern is almost certainly going to be present, likely to be foremost in their minds, and deal with it as outlined above. Know that you must help them get past it quickly and comfortably and you can do so by simply not attempting to sell them anything. This means not trying to convince, persuade, etc., as to anything. This isn't just in relation to purchasing particular financial products; it is in relation to anything, including your services. Trying to convince a perspective client to hire you is "selling" just as assuredly as is trying to convince a perspective client to invest in a particular investment product.

Obviously, you desire to have a perspective client engage your services. While it may seem counterintuitive, the thing most likely to dissuade them is trying to persuade them to do so. So, what is your option? What do you do instead? You simply layout what you offer, your services, how you work, what your processes are, and how you are compensated. Then you convey the actual criteria you use to determine whether or not you take someone as a client. Immediately, the conversation will often shift to your perspective client trying to convince you that they qualify, rather than them resisting attempts on your part to get them to say yes.

Actual criteria is the critical element here, because if you attempt to set up some phony criteria and then take everyone whose breath will fog a mirror, you are going to shoot yourself in the foot. Intelligent people with money and life experience will see through this. They will either see what is happening, or they will just get an uncomfortable feeling in the interaction. Either way, they will leave with your card and company brochure and say, "Let us think about this and we will get back to you", and then they won't. Been there; done that; got that T-shirt. The worst part of that scenario is that they miss the opportunity to take advantage of all that you could have done for them, and it is actually decided before they ever leave your desk.

Sharing what you do, giving them your criteria, and not personally identifying in the least with what they do or don't do, will change your posture in this business. It will result in an immediate increase in the number of prospective clients who become clients and ultimately implement with you. More importantly, it will change how you feel internally as a professional.

Explain to clients how you work — which never includes trying to sell them — and then honor your promise. Explain your process to your client, so they will know what to expect. Let them know that you aren't interested in wasting time with people who will waste your time. Tell them that your criteria for taking new clients was established because your time is valuable and it has to be protected for the benefit of those people who understand what you do and that you do take as clients.

The following list is how I inform clients coming to my office of my process, and what each step will achieve for them:

- I will give you a checklist of items that I will need you to bring me (no forms to complete and no questions to answer).

- You will bring in all your financial information.

- I will help you determine and formalize your financial objectives. This is where there are questions, but I will ask them and I will record the answers.

- I will arrange all your information into a format with which I can work.

- I will uncover relevant parameters of which you aren't currently apprised.

- I am going to show you what might happen, what you hope will happen, but what could happen to you and your family if you leave things as they are.

- I am then going to reveal any current potential dangers, red flags, problems, exposures, or vulnerabilities I find.

- I will unveil and share with you strategies designed to overcome undesired parameters.

- I will provide you with available options, the first of which will always be to leave things as they are.

- I will help you implement any changes you want to make.

- We are going to meet at least annually to review and update your financial objectives and your current plan.

- Keep in mind that I am never in charge at my desk; you are.

This is a concise outline. You'll want to adapt the content and layout to reflect your own processes. However you decide to implement this, know that outlining the work process puts your prospective clients at ease. As you go through the process, you can literally see the expression on their faces change as defensive, resistant mindsets dissolve. They are always expecting a sales effort and they relax when it doesn't come. They simply know what to expect and they are comfortable with the process as it plays out.

As long as they are feeling, "What are you selling, I don't want any," they are incapable of making informed decisions. None of us can function properly with that mindset. However, considering their state of mind and functioning accordingly helps to eliminate barriers, and critically important, doesn't erect new ones. Thus, they can properly evaluate what you have to offer. This serves their real financial best interests and doesn't waste your time or theirs with resistive, destructive attitudes. Of course, as we now know, their best interest is your best interest. By helping clients glide gently into a receptive mindset by simply focusing on potential pitfalls and options, they are automatically "coachable". They want improvements, and your "no sales pitch" approach towards financial advising has a far greater chance of allowing and resulting in improvements for them.

The above is important, however, it isn't the most important part of helping your clients feel safe with you. In our industry, unless you offer nothing but FDIC Insured investment vehicles, which aren't going to compete for potential performance and tax advantage, you can't help your clients feel safe by promising them they won't lose money. You can't promise them their accounts won't fluctuate or even be volatile.

What you can do to help them feel safe is to acknowledge risks specifically and succinctly. I heard once that if I want to help you believe what I am going to tell you, it helps if I will first tell you three things that you already know to be true, and then tell you what I want you to believe. *Clients know investing comes with risk.* Therefore, rather than avoiding the subject, or downplaying risk which may manifest itself, you want to specifically address it and state the obvious. Never sidestep the subject of risk! With every investment, you bring it up, disclose the type of risk, and how you think it compares in extent to other investment options, those you offer and those you don't, including the ones they already have.

Again, it might seem counterintuitive, but disclosing risk doesn't keep people from taking it. It prevents them taking undisclosed risks, an objective we all share. Our clients all took risks before they met us and they expect to continue to do so. Disclosing risks (that they know are there, anyway) simply builds our clients' confidence in us, and feel safer with us because they now know we are being honest with them.

A little side effect of disclosing risks is that it obviates the need for apologies or to salvage relationships after the risk manifests itself, an uncomfortable conversation for clients and advisors alike. Have the conversation now and you don't have to apologize for it when it comes. When the thing we told them could go down the tubes goes down the tubes, the conversation is, "Well, we just had one of those worse case scenarios we talked about!" You want the initial disclosure to be full and complete, if anything, overstated and dramatic. If they only lost 70% of the money they invested in that account, the conversation is, "Remember when we talked about the possibility of this losing every-thing invested…? Well, this one almost did it.!" Neither you nor your clients will like it, but your relationship will be stronger than ever, and, more importantly, you won't feel guilty!

Clearly and specifically disclosing risk doesn't reduce clients' will-ingness to do business with you - it increases it. In some cases, it results in their agreement to other, different financial vehicles, but those are the cases where the different financial vehicle was the appropriate one. If a client isn't willing to take a specific risk, the time to determine that is before they take it! Also, a client insisting on less risk doesn't mean they don't do business with you. It probably means they won't make as much money as your other clients, but that is their choice. They are still your clients.

Helping your clients fire a former advisor

Most of the prospective clients you meet already have a financial advisor of some description. Eventually, if they decide to engage you as their advisor, they will have to fire their old advisor. For most people, once they grasp that it is in their best interest to fire someone, they can and will do it. This next statement is critical. **The hard part for most clients isn't firing their current advisor; it is _making the decision to fire their current advisor._** Once they have made the decision to do it, their own self-interest makes doing it not only easy, but natural and automatic. After all, they don't really have a vested interest in the relationship. I have discovered over the years, however, that **_deciding to do it - is what's emotionally challenging_**.

Helping your clients _get past the decision_ to move their accounts from a former advisor is an extreme act of client consideration. My suggestion is to help them do it without ever having them experience the sense of being on the spot to make that decision. In other words, **_help them fire their advisor without ever actually deciding to fire their advisor._** This may seem like it would be challenging, but is actually remarkably easy to do, and astonishingly effective. Here is how you help your client do this:

- **Introduce the idea of separation early.** You may want to introduce the idea of termination early in your relationship; sometimes as early as the first meeting if it is going well, as was the case with one of my new clients several years ago, where I literally stumbled onto this remarkable client consideration protocol.

Gloria, my prospective client, had a substantial portfolio. For the last twenty years, she had relied on the advice and counsel of a financial advisor at her local bank branch. Her portfolio had grown over the years, and she wasn't unhappy with the advisor.

However, as she approached retirement, she wanted the security of knowing she would have enough money to see her through her golden years. In our first meeting, she shared with me that while she had made money during a long stretch of good economic conditions, as things were, she was worried about the future state of the economy and the market in general. She had experienced ups and downs and wasn't comfortable with the same level of volatility during her retirement years that she had experienced while growing her assets. She wasn't convinced that what had worked in the past would continue to work in the future. She had mentioned this concern to her current advisor, but he had not addressed it. His comment was that "the market has always come back". Don't ever assume that all is well with an account or with a relationship, just because the account has made money or because there is a long-standing relationship. I think, later proved to be an accurate assessment, that her advisor had made the critical error of either failing to listen to his client or failing to give what that client said appropriate weight.

By the way, in more than twenty years of "missing the boat" in my own career, I had made the same mistake. Other advisors had the luxury of benefiting from my mistakes, not because I wrote a book they could read, but because they got my clients! I was the guy failing to pay appropriate attention to what my clients were telling me!

Although it was early in our relationship, I said to Gloria, "Gloria, once we have spent some time together in the process I use for all of my clients, whether you keep everything exactly where it is, change everything, or something in between, is going to be your call. Your first choice is always going to be to leave things as they are. The fact that I do the analysis we have discussed and give you some feedback doesn't mean you have to change anything. However, should you decide that what we discuss is better than what you have now, you will find yourself at a decision point. You will have to either maintain a relationship with your current financial advisor… or do what you feel is in the best interest of you and your family."

"This isn't something you need to concern yourself with now", I told Gloria in that early conversation. You don't have the information yet on which that decision could be made; in other words, you don't know at this point whether or not you would have any reason to make any changes. I just want you to be aware that it is possible that you are going to arrive at that juncture. It helps you if you are already prepared for the possibility that in the next few days or weeks, this is where you may find yourself, and you may want to begin thinking about how you would feel about that."

After sharing this with Gloria, I shifted the conversation back to her data gathering and fact finding, and helping her formalize her objectives. At our next meeting, I revealed optional strategies available to her (notice I did not say *recommendations*) relative to her risk tolerance concerns. I also reviewed her account titles and beneficiary designations, and shared with her how, as her financial affairs were currently structured, her children would be required to spend months with assets tied up in probate, and that we were going to restructure her account titling to avoid this dilemma. I also explained that most of this was going to be done without additional costs, using the account titling with simple Payable on Death and Transfer on Death registrations and through the use of custom designed beneficiary designations, including Primary, Contingent, Second Contingent, and For the Benefit Of (FBO) designations for minor beneficiaries. When we moved into the implementation stage of the process, I mentioned something about the other advisor. Gloria quickly replied, "Oh, that isn't a problem. Remember, we talked about that the last time I was here." I suddenly realized that *what had actually happened was that Gloria went from, "I may have to make that decision" to "That decision has already been made" without ever actually having to experience the emotions that come with making that challenging decision!* She had considered the possibility, forgotten about it, and then, with all of the advantages of making the transition to what we were offering in front of her, she was taking the position that she had already made that decision.

I acknowledge that I stumbled onto that strategy while working with Gloria, but I have used it many times since, exactly as described – and I have yet to have it fail! Using this process, clients will do the appropriate thing, but they don't find themselves in the uncomfortable position of having *to decide* to fire someone. It's like magic. Somehow, they actually go from "OK, I get it. I might have to consider that possibility" to "I have already decided that" without ever actually putting themselves on the spot to make the decision.

Considerately seed the notion of the availability of something better for your client and their families, before the time comes to make the decision, and remind them, specifically, that they do not need to make that decision now. This allows your new client to comfortably weigh his or her options personally and privately. Then deliver those things that are better!

Key to this process is the inclusion of the additional advantages of your work that their old advisor wasn't providing, and, in fact, never addressed. That advisor didn't provide POD and TOD account registrations, custom beneficiary designations, and other key parameters that would save his client's families thousands of dollars, all the while not costing a cent to implement.

The combination of these added value services, and the introduction of the idea of making an improvement before the decision is to be made allows your prospective client to weigh these now obvious advantages that have surfaced during your process. But it also allows them to move forward through the transition without getting bogged down in an irrelevant sense of remorse for their old advisor, and without any natural resistance that would have been created by efforts to persuade on your part.

You will likely find that when the subject comes up again, your new client is already past the problem; they have already covered that in their minds. My experience is that they don't realize when they made the decision, because they never made the decision. By the time the subject comes up again, they are likely to have subconsciously already done what is in their best interest, without ever having to labor over it, to struggle with the decision. In this way, you take the sting out of the process - just one more example of extreme client consideration on your part.

I have been taught by the financial industry that building relationships is the way to get and keep clients. I have been taught by experience with clients, however, that the value of that relationship in their minds will wane every time, as soon as they understand that it is in their best interest to do something more advantageous. Again, every time you consider your client with what you do for them that the "so-called" competition isn't doing, you enhance the likelihood that they will bring you their accounts. Now, not only are they comfortable with the process of you giving them options, they "feel good" about taking the initiative for action. As a result, it is more likely that they will graduate to a higher level of financial functioning, because it is in their best interest to do so.

A prospective client doesn't have the emotional ammunition to go to his current financial advisor and make a case for changing financial directions because he likes you better. He has no need for ammunition at all to notify his ex-advisor that he has taken some intelligent steps that better secures his, his surviving spouse's, and his family's financial well-being. It doesn't hurt anything to make the process for doing so comfortable.

Note that we aren't likely to ever have this happen because we recommended a potentially better investment vehicle, or showed them the need for life insurance. Financial products don't do that and their old advisor already showed them financial products. Other than "developing rapport" and "breaking the ice" small talk, it may have been all they talked about. But when you helped prevent the eventuality of their surviving family members spending $350-$400/hour for months on end in the estate transfer process, they realize on their own that they need to do something about this problem. They will naturally and comfortably transition to an advisor who helps them do this and other things not previously addressed.

• **Don't make their previous advisor a bad guy for not doing for his clients what you are going to do for them i.e. for not being at the same advanced level that you are.** The next step comes when your clients tell you they want to work with you. This is your opportunity to help them with the actual separation from their previous advisor, but remember: this is someone your new clients like. This is not the "enemy". This is a respected professional, who has integrity, who has served his or her client to the best of his or her ability, who is honorably working to make a living and provide for his or her family. Give the current advisor credit for previous accomplishments, and assist your clients as they "graduate" to the next level of the financial planning process.

I tell my clients: "Your previous advisor helped you accumulate assets. He was supposed to help you accumulate assets. That was his job, he got paid for doing it, it was appropriate that he do so, and he did a good job of what he agreed to do. It is the fact that you've accumulated assets that will allow you to take advantage of the higher-level, tax-efficient distribution strategies that we are going to employ. You were at one level of the financial planning process before you met (their advisor). You were at another level while you were working with him. It is only appropriate that you now graduate to the next level".

Everyone likes to graduate! Moving up is always a desirable step. Since your clients took advantage of the strategies available in the last phase, why wouldn't they take advantage of available improvements in their current phase? This approach is comfortable and positive, rather than confrontational and combative.

- **Write the 'Dear John' letter for your clients.** When your new clients elect to engage your services over those of a previous advisor, assist them by writing a letter for them in which they thank the previous advisor for their success to date. This letter will do much more than dismiss a previous advisor. This letter will reinforce the decision in the client's mind and it will, again, differentiate between what they have been doing and what they are now doing. By incorporating into the letter a list of what you are doing that is different, it takes the fight out of the other advisor and it reminds your clients of why they are making the change. See Exhibit G – Ex-Financial Advisor Letter.

Exhibit G – Ex-Financial Advisor Letter

April 14, 2015

Ira Closer

Investment Product Sales, Inc.

100 East Bay Street

Jacksonville, FL 32202

Dear Ira:

I am writing to advise you that June and I have made the decision to restructure our financial affairs, and in doing so, will be closing our IPS, Inc. account. We want to thank you and want you to know that our decision is not a result of any dissatisfaction with you or your services. June and I have engaged the services of a firm which, in addition to handling our investments, is assisting us in implementing a complete financial, tax, and estate plan. We are structuring things so as to reduce our market risk, secure our retirement income, and minimize our income taxes. We are also executing a trust that will help us make certain that our assets will avoid probate, go to our children and grandchildren, even should the survivor of the two of us remarry, and protect assets from our children's divorcing spouses should that ever be the case. Additionally, they are retitling all of our non-trust owned accounts and creating custom beneficiary designation letters, helping us to assure those assets avoid probate and go where we want them to go with minimal cost, delay, and hassle for our family.

We have signed the necessary paperwork to transfer our accounts and would appreciate your assistance in making certain there are no delays in initiating immediate implementation. We have given this a great deal of thought; we know this to be not only in our best interest, but that of our children and our grandchildren as well.

Again, we genuinely appreciate your help and wish you the very best in your career.

Respectfully,

(Client Name)
(Client Address)
(Client City, State Zip)
(Client Phone Number)

If this letter doesn't reflect services you offer, either modify it accordingly, or perhaps add the services delineated in this letter to your offerings. A great deal of thought went into the design of this letter. One reason it is so effective in preventing substantial effort on the part of the current advisor to retain his relationship with his client is that it reflects services he is not providing and it leaves him with both the intellectual and emotional sense that he isn't qualified to compete. His impression is that his client has graduated to a higher standard of financial advice and he willingly acquiesces. In many cases the current advisor, himself, will actually understand that this is a good move for your clients. When this happens, and there isn't a fight, you don't have to worry about winning the fight.

The other intended and realized result is that this letter reiterates once and again, and reinforces for your new client, what you are doing for them and the enhanced value it provides compared to where they were before they met you. Even again, they see that the decision they have made is a prudent one; it reflects specifically what they are doing and that it is a good thing that they are doing it. It doesn't just help them ease past a potentially difficult project; it solidifies the relationship between you and your client based on concrete undisputable parameters, further solidifying your client's new relationship with you just at the point where an old advisor might otherwise want to challenge it.

To write this letter for your clients, you must first know what it is about your practice that is better than what they previously had. Looking for and adding value to your services makes what you do more valuable for your clients, makes it easier to communicate reasons they should use you, and makes the construction of this letter easy. But, understand that it is the whole picture of your practice that is reflected in this letter. If you are looking for additional ways to add value to your practice, check our website for future books.

• **Prepare them for 'the call.'** In case it does come, advise your clients to expect a phone call from their previous advisor attempting to dissuade them from their decision. Remind them that they may be making improvements, but he is losing a client. He might suggest that he could do for them what you are proposing. Remind them that, while well intentioned and obviously disappointed to be losing their business, if he actually could have done all of this for them, he reasonably would have already done so during the period of time he was working with them. After all, he did have all the years he worked with them to suggest it. He may try to denigrate the direction you are taking them. Tell them ahead of time that this is what advisors say when they don't know what else to say. Suggest that they simply go back to the content of the letter they sent explaining the decision (make certain they have a copy). Additionally, suggest that they convey that the decision has been made and that it would be a great consideration to them if he would help them effect the transfer. This will leave your new clients prepared for what is coming and they will handle it appropriately.

- **Clients are often surprised when that call doesn't come.**
Clients are very surprised when their discharged advisor doesn't even respond, but for two reasons I am not. One is that it lends itself to the commoditization so prevalent in our industry. The client was very worried about ending what for them was a personal relationship, but for their previous advisor was not. They had a relationship – he didn't!

Secondly, when the advisor's sense is that the client has moved from a product sales relationship (his) to a true financial planning relationship (yours), he can't bring himself to object. Often, the advisor will recognize that the client has found someone who is actually doing what he, himself, has always aspired to do, but hasn't implemented in his or her practice. They know that there are advisors out there who actually do financial, tax, and estate planning, and they don't see themselves competing when one of those advisors come into the picture. They don't feel capable of competing.

If it sounds like I am being egotistical here, please believe me; I am not. I was that advisor for too many years to break my arm patting myself on the back. It is only the fact that I have graduated that allows me to now be on the sending end of that letter – I used to get those letters!

Helping your client separate from a previous advisor comfortably is another facet of client consideration at its best. By having this conversation with your clients before that call comes, you identify and confront a stumbling block your client may face, and help them prepare for it and then get past it. Don't leave your new clients hanging out there to "deal with it as best they can", without tools to handle it, and hope it goes to your advantage. Train them before it happens, and help your clients get through it comfortably! At this point in the process, preparing them for what comes next is client consideration at its best.

Increasing the chances that prospective clients will get past the initial interview

We have talked extensively about not discussing financial products in the first meeting. Now we are going to take this idea a little further, in a way that is just as important, but a little more subtle.

Assume that after hearing you speak at their Rotary Club[17] meeting, a prospective client visits your office. After spending some time learning who he is, and what his retirement objectives are, he finally says to you, "What I am most interested in is making sure my intended heirs get what I leave them". (Incidentally this is a great topic for speaking engagements.)

With all the subtlety you can muster you tell your prospective client "It's going to be important that as we address your estate plan, we also consider your investment portfolio to make sure it's structured properly for your retirement objectives." However, what he hears is "Ok, we can help you protect your assets for your children and grandchildren, but we have to sell you some investments in the process." Then you can't figure out why he never came back, or why, at best, he was resistant to your suggestions, and you had to close like crazy to get him to take recommended action you knew was good for him.

Based on your experience as a financial advisor, you can see very early in the discussions that there are gaps in the design of his asset allocation model, no one has even addressed distribution strategies, and, left as is, he will pay more income taxes before and during retirement than is required. You also know that with the right approach and after gently helping him get these issues on the table, your services will likely be engaged, aiding him in the solutions for these glaring problems.

---

17   www.rotaryinternational.com

In other words, it is blatantly obvious to you that this person needs your help with more than just tweaking his estate plan – what he came to you for. Additionally, speaking candidly, you know that you don't get paid for helping him tweak his estate plan, but you would be compensated on the investment side if you repositioned his current investment account assets.

As an experienced advisor, however, it would be most inconsiderate of your client and of you to discuss any of this following his comments to you as to why he is at your desk. At this point in your, currently tenuous relationship, these subjects are as much "off the table" as financial products! Why? Because his current topic of interest is asset protection, probate avoidance, and protecting against unintended heirs, exactly what you talked about at the Rotary meeting. Also, he is expecting you to try to realign his investment portfolio (that is translated as "try to sell him something") and he will automatically and naturally resist this. He is not yet of a mindset to consider these changes.

What you want to do at this juncture is to spend some time getting to know him. While gathering the data, you can ask probing questions relative to retirement and his investment portfolio, but only as it relates to asset protection, probate avoidance, and the existing possibility of unintended heirs.

You can help him get a clear picture of his daughter's husband divorcing her three years after his death, and taking half of what he left her. You can discuss retirement assets, but as they relate to assets that will provide for his surviving spouse while protected from her new husband! Work toward that complete picture, but only as it relates to what he came in to talk to you about.

After you help him solve and prevent the problems about which he is concerned, he will graciously engage in conversation about other issues. You have now clearly demonstrated your value as a trusted advisor, and have not pounced on him like a part-time used car salesman!

When you develop an itemized list (Balance Sheet) for the purpose of addressing individual account titles and payable on death designations and custom beneficiary designations for each related asset, you will have a complete picture of everything he owns. A conversation to address additional concerns will flow naturally, later. At that point, you have done something for him that no other advisor has ever done, and it is so much more likely that he will allow you to engage him in conversation about investment options that are more tax advantaged, or that incorporate distribution strategies that will benefit him and his family. Replacing those "fill in the blank" beneficiary designation forms and their potential gaps with custom designed documents you provide builds a foundation on which you can easily and comfortably build an investment advisory relationship. The statements he provided in the asset protection process told you everything you needed to know or at least opened the door to discuss his investment portfolio.

The considerate thing to do at a first meeting is to determine if there are specific concerns that brought you this potential client and to address those concerns. Devote this meeting to discussing the processes you use to address the problem your client came in to discuss with you; that which was foremost in her mind. *It is OK if you know that you are going to give them some input as to their retirement portfolio; it isn't necessary to tell them so at this point.*

By concentrating on the topic in which the prospective client had expressed a specific interest, you also protect the opportunity to address everything else later (once you have determined objectives and gathered her data). How do I know? I know this because I did it the wrong way hundreds of times over a period of years, losing clients before they became clients, and wondering what went wrong? Remember the mirror – it was showing me myself – I just wasn't paying attention!

Casually mentioning that you will review their entire financial, tax, and estate situation is appropriate later in the planning process, but not initially. Trying to make a case for clients changing anything other than what they told you is on their mind is inconsiderate, and even introducing it too early can prevent any potential opportunities to address more with them in the future. There will come a time when there is no resistance to those retirement portfolio discussions; but they will be much better received, after you have already solved the problem they came to you to discuss.

This leaves one final element left to unveil in the planning process - implementation, known in the industry as "closing the deal". This is such a vital element in the process that I have reserved its discussion for the final chapter, as its role within the process of Client Consideration is significant, and will bring full circle your understanding of everything learned within these pages. As you will see, before you read Chapter Nine, it is very important, necessary actually, that you have a firm grasp on the Chapters One - Eight before you read it.

CHAPTER NINE

Implementation

Everything you need to know about "closing" is in Chapter One through Chapter Eight. Implementation is the simplest part of the equation if you have a "Client Consideration" based practice. When the time to implement comes, you stand up and say, "Let's go to Sue's office. Sue doesn't let me do paperwork around here. She did once and said, "Never again!" Then you escort your clients to your assistant's office where she does the paperwork.

The point is that if you have been considerate of your clients in all the ways we have discussed, there is no "closing". There is no "overcoming objections". "Closing Techniques" aren't needed. Before your client could object, you've already found out what your client wanted, and put it and only it on the table. I once interviewed a financial advisor for the possibility of him joining my practice. In the interview, he said, "Hal, I am pretty good at overcoming objections". My reply was, "Mark, anything your client objects to shouldn't be in the plan".

Don't learn how to close – learn how to not have to close. Build a plan with an asset allocation model that makes sense, that covers the bases, that your clients want to implement. Long before you get to implementation, you will know if you are on the right track or need to regroup. Don't learn how to close – instead, consider your clients and learn how to not have to close. Implementation is the natural result of the strategic planning process if that process is carried out from beginning to end based on consideration for your client. You will know you are doing it right when you don't have to "close".

Conclusion

Each of us has a marketing program that introduces our firm and our processes to new prospective clients. We have a model we use to develop financial plans. We have asset allocation models. We have a client-service program to handle follow-up service requests for our clients. If you will spend a little time developing an overall Client Consideration program for your office, you will change the tone of your practice and will automatically get more in touch and in tune with your prospective clients and clients. Your staff will become more client focused. Client consideration isn't a marketing tool - it is marketing replacement. Client consideration isn't based on the question, "Will this make my client buy from me?" It is based on the questions, "Does this work better financially for my client?" "Does this help my prospective client feel more comfortable in our first interview?" "Does this help my client in the interaction, having nothing to do with whether or not he purchases something I am offering?" "Does this add value to the relationship that other advisors in my area aren't providing?" "Does this help my client move from "What are you selling – I don't want any!" to "How do we make all this happen?"

In the final analysis, there is nothing you can do for your client that is more considerate than helping them move from "What are you selling? I don't want any!" to "So how do we make this happen?" Everything you can do to assist your client make that shift is considerate of your client. Find what those things are and provide them. It starts with recognizing that is where they are. It includes providing the right "controllable" solutions and disclosing "uncontrollable" parameters. It ends with taking care of them after they make the decision to implement the strategies you have provided.

Parenthetically, clients who are truly considered do business much more readily than those who aren't. It is the natural progression of things – It is how you function, personally, when you go shopping. Clients can tell the difference between a client consideration based practice and a selling based practice. Some clients will buy from selling based practices, probably enough to keep you in business and allow you to pay your bills, but it isn't enjoyable; it isn't personally rewarding. Way down deep inside you, it isn't any fun. One process increases resistance, and we can learn to overcome resistance; but the other one helps people move comfortably to wanting to make improvements they believe will help them, avoiding resistance. One process will pay the bills; and the other will move you in a positive direction towards self-actualization where everything needed is provided.

Every advisor wants more clients, bigger clients, and a higher implementation ratio. If we advisors would learn to take care of, to more effectively serve, the clients we have, the other objectives would take care of themselves. True client consideration results in more than plan implementation. It results in a higher degree of differentiation between you and selling based financial advisors in your neighborhood, and much more importantly, a greater sense of confidence on your part as you move into the next relationship with a desired client. It is the paradox in our business that "not selling" results in more sales than does "selling".

Every successful financial service provider must see their clients as a primary factor in their success, for without client's financial needs and objectives driving demand…they'd have no one to whom they could deliver financial services. The other primary factor is themselves, how they, personally, approach their industry. For most financial service providers, it is a given that they want to "do the right thing" by our clients. But the right thing, that which takes us to where we want to be, isn't limited to not cheating our clients! When I was totally asleep to everything in these pages, I had integrity – I wanted to do the right thing. That simply isn't enough. It is very possible, even likely, that we are in fact, asleep. We can be totally asleep to the factors that are influencing our business, driving or hindering our progress.

We came to the playing field desiring to achieve financial success, to be beneficial to our clients, and to contribute to our industry. Over the years I have witnessed countless financial planners and advisors alike; work harder and harder on their marketing skills, because that is what the industry teaches us to do. Planning models, educational programs, and other resources and tools came into play, but as we tried to find the advantage, or even just the connection needed to "breakthrough", the emphasis was always on marketing.

This seemed reasonable enough – the accepted consensus being that marketing drives sales and sales drive revenue, but for those first twenty years, I could never find a real "truth", an "answer". Everything I read always held the promise of the answer on the next page, but for more than twenty years, it just wasn't there.

> **For me the breakthrough was the realization that my clients' best interest is my best interest.**

It was just that simple, and everything in this book stemmed from that realization.

This book mentions obtaining clients who already have financial advisors. Those advisors need to lose those clients - a client leaving is just a reflection of that advisor in the mirror. That advisor may or may not ever know what happened, but the opportunity is there. The only chance that the advisor will figure it out is if he or she understands that they are responsible for their results, if he or she is just willing to check the mirror, objectively.

On the other hand, client consideration based advisors aren't worried about you taking their clients – those clients aren't up for grabs! They know that they are their only competition and you are your only competition. If all advisors would build client consideration based practices, more people would use financial advisors – there are enough clients to go around.

As financial advisors, we attempt so many things to improve our practice, The simple truth is that you can't improve your practice without doing something better for your clients. Forget marketing, forget selling; devote your focus solely to more and better ways to serve your clients. Your clients will take care of you.

In writing "The Financial Advisor's Guide to Client Consideration", I wanted to share something that was universal, something that could be used by every advisor. I wanted to offer something that was a real "truth", a constant. I wanted to offer a solution that can work for everyone equally (not product specific), and something that leaves behind a lasting contribution for the work invested into it.

Education and resources will always be important to what you do, but tools are just tools. There is obvious value in staying current and up to date with industry offerings, products and services, and your practice will not be successful without long-lasting relationships with your clients. But the true measure of your success, of that of your practice, is the value of what you do for your clients, what you bring to the table that they didn't have before they met you. This is what will craft a continual progression of better prospective clients and clients. Additionally, we may have been conditioned to overrate educational (extrinsic) resources. My experience is that it is by turning inward to an intrinsic resource, that I found my answer to building a sustainable element in my practice and a personal perspective I could respect.

All esoteric teaching says that the answers we seek are within us. Perhaps something said herein will result in a chance look inside you. If so, you will find the most incredible being, longing not only to be served i.e. with success in the business, but to serve. This is the thing that makes this business worthwhile, the thing that makes it personally satisfying. If, perchance, this book helps you find it, and release it to serve you the way it wants to, then it was worth the time it took to write it. I always knew there was an answer; I just didn't know that the mirror was the teacher! I don't purport to be your teacher, but if I can shortcut the trial and tribulation phase just a little, then this book will be worth the price you paid many times over and the space it takes on your nightstand.

Final Note: It has to have occurred to you as you have read this book that every time we discussed client consideration and things you can do that work better for your clients, there were obvious benefits to you. That should not be surprising. I suggested that your best interest is your client's best interest. If this is true, doesn't it have to be true that your client's best interest is your best interest? First year algebra: If A = B, then B = A.

Look further, though and really bring this teaching home as it is intended. You could do all of these things with a "What's in it for me?" attitude. You could do all of these things with a "social worker wearing a white hat" attitude. Or you could do all of these things understanding that there isn't a difference; there is only one anything and it is everything. Your client is you; you are your client. This creates the best possible internal sense of you – what I consider the ultimate human objective.

Tell me whatever it is that you want and I will remind you that you want it because you sense that if you have it, you will feel better than you would without it! Feeling good is the ultimate objective. As much time as we spend in our professional endeavors, why not engage in them in a way that feels good? Taking care of our clients really feels good!

Wishing you the absolute best in your financial advisory career. I hope it will lead to where mine took me.

Your fellow advisor

Hal

There are some resources I consider imperative for a financial advisor to utilize:

One is Ed Slott's Elite IRA Advisor Group. Learn the ropes on IRA's and qualified plans. There is so much I didn't know in this area that I have learned from Ed that I feel fortunate that I didn't inadvertently cost a client major consequences before I met Ed. See IRAHELP.com.

Going through the Oechsli (Oxley) Institute's Rainmaker Training has done more to help me change my perspective relative to working with higher net worth clients than anything else in my career. See www.oechsli.com.

I first subscribed to economist, Harry Dent's, resources because I thought he could tell me what was going to happen. Fortunately, before it was too late for my clients, I discovered that he had, instead, helped shape the way I look at our economy and make my own decisions. See http://harrydent.com.

There are three books that have had a noticeable impact on my ability to meet and attract clients with whom I want to work without spending horrendous amounts of money on "marketing".

They are:

"Start With Why" by Simon Senek, Publisher: Portfolio, a member of Penguin Group

"The One Thing" by Gary Keller, Publisher: Bard Press (NY)

"The Little Black Book of Connections" by Jeffrey Gitomer Publisher: Simon & Schuster

I recommend reading them in the above order.
Hal Rogers

To contact Hal w/ questions about anything in this book, email him at: hal@gtfjax.com.

CPSIA information can be obtained
at www.ICGtesting.com
Printed in the USA
BVOW06*1841010218
506986BV00005B/8/P

9 781478 738145